RIJKSMUSEUM AMSTERDAM

Highlights from the collection

RIJKSMUSEUM AMSTERDAM
Highlights from the collection
was published by the Rijksmuseum-Stichting.

The introductions to the various sections were
written by the heads of the departments
concerned.
Paintings: *Wouter Kloek*
Sculpture and Decorative Arts: *Reinier Baarsen*
Dutch History: *Wim Vroom*
The Print Room: *Peter Schatborn*
Asiatic Art: *Pauline Lunsingh Scheurleer*

The captions are by *Marleen Dominicus-van
Soest, Judikje Kiers* and *Fieke Tissink*

Coordination: *Theo Schoenmaker*
Assistant-coordinator: *Liesbeth van Noortwijk*
Final editing: *Annemarie Vels Heijn*

Translation: *Babel, Utrecht*

All photographs were taken by the Rijksmuseum's
Photographic Department

Design: *Loek de Leeuw, Inmerc bv*
Lithography: *Nederlof Repro, Cruquius Heemstede*
Typesetting and printing: *bv Kunstdrukkerij
Mercurius-Wormerveer*
Binder: *Spiegelenberg BV*
(*onderdeel* van *de Molier Groep*)
Paper: *Hello Gloss, wood-free glazed machine coated
paper 150 gr/m², produced by Sappi, from the
Bührmann-Ubbens Papier collection*
Project realization and distribution: *Inmerc bv,
Wormer*

RIJKSMUSEUM AMSTERDAM

Highlights from the collection

RIJKS MUSEUM
amsterdam

TABLE OF CONTENTS

Originally known as the National Art Gallery, the Rijksmuseum was opened to the public in 1800. At first it was located in the Huis ten Bosch palace in The Hague, and the collection mainly consisted of paintings. In 1808 the museum moved to Amsterdam, where it was initially housed in the Palace on the Dam and later in the Trippenhuis on Kloveniersburgwal.

The museum finally moved to its current premises in 1885. At this point the Dutch Museum of History and Art (previously located in The Hague) was merged with the Rijksmuseum, thus laying the foundations for today's Dutch History and Sculpture and Decorative Arts collections. In 1898 and from 1906 to 1919, a number of extensions were made to the south side of the building, creating what is now known as the South Wing. Between 1962 and 1969, the available exhibition space was considerably increased by building new three-storey structures in the museum's two inner courtyards.

Since 1885, the Rijksmuseum's collection has comprised Dutch painting from the fifteenth to the nineteenth century, Dutch and foreign prints and drawings from the same period, Dutch history from the Middle Ages onwards, and Sculpture and Decorative Arts (furniture, glass, silver, porcelain, ceramics, jewellery, costumes and textiles) from the Middle Ages to the nineteenth century. Over the years, modest groups of paintings by foreign artists have been added to the collection; at the same time, the Decorative Arts department has acquired an increasingly international outlook and has extended its collection to include the opening decades of the twentieth century. In 1952, the Museum of Asiatic Art was set up in the Rijksmuseum building, and since then the Rijksmuseum has comprised the following five departments: Paintings, Sculpture and Decorative Arts, Dutch History, the Print Room and Asiatic Art. Each department has its own exhibition rooms, although the History and Decorative Arts departments also contain a large number of paintings.

The Rijksmuseum is the Dutch national museum of old art and history, and as such it is the largest museum in the country.

The Rijksmuseum's collection of paintings by the great seventeenth-century Dutch masters is world-famous. Frans Hals, Johannes Vermeer, Jan van Goyen, Jacob van Ruisdael, Pieter Saenredam and Jan Steen are popular with the general public for their portraits, interiors, landscapes, churches and scenes of revelry. And above all, of course, it is Rembrandt – renowned for his mastery of light and shade – who attracts so many visitors to the Rijksmuseum. Not only does the Rijksmuseum possess a number of outstanding works by this great master, including *The Night Watch, The Syndics* and *The Jewish Bride,* but its total of 19 Rembrandts is a representative selection of the artist's work. The Paintings department provides a chronological picture of the Netherlandish school of painting from the fifteenth to the end of the nineteenth century, in some cases with particular emphasis on certain schools, themes or individual artists.

This selection of Dutch painting begins with early specimens from the fifteenth and sixteenth century, including work by such artists as Geertgen tot Sint Jans, Lucas van Leyden and Pieter Aertsen. After this come paintings by the seventeenth-century masters. A typical characteristic of Dutch painters is that they mostly concentrated on particular kinds of paintings or 'genres'. For example, Hendrick Avercamp specialized in winter landscapes, Pieter Claesz in still lifes, Frans Hals in portraits, and Esaias van de Velde and Jan van Goyen in depictions of the Dutch landscape. Pieter Saenredam excelled in church interiors, and Pieter de Hooch and Johannes Vermeer owe their fame to their renderings of domestic interiors. Later landscape painters included a group of artists – among them Aelbert Cuyp – whose forte was Italianate landscapes in the late afternoon light. Jacob van Ruisdael, who became famous for his cloudy skies, took his themes from the landscapes of Holland and Scandinavia. The Rijksmuseum's hall of fame contains groups of paintings from the second half of the seventeenth century. These include seascapes by the elder and younger Van de Velde and works by direct associates of Rembrandt's, such as Ferdinand Bol and Philips Koninck. Later works by Rembrandt himself, including *The Jewish Bride* and *The Syndics,* are also displayed here.

The South Wing contains paintings from the eighteenth and nineteenth century. In addition to a selection of works by eighteenth-century masters, with particular emphasis on Cornelis Troost, there is a small collection of selected pastels. Constantly changing selections from the museum's extensive collection of nineteenth-century Dutch masters are likewise on display, alternately emphasizing the Romantic school (with landscapes by artists such as Barend Cornelis Koekkoek and Andreas Schelfhout), the Hague and Amsterdam Schools (represented by artists including Jacob and Matthijs Maris, Anton Mauve, Isaac Israëls and George Breitner) or other items such as the collection of foreign masters (including works by Gustave Courbet, James McNeill Whistler and others).

The national art collection, which came into being in 1795, originally consisted of works confiscated from the exiled House of Orange, but was soon to be significantly extended by King Louis Napoleon. Over the years, considerable parts of the art collection of the city of Amsterdam came into the museum's possession. Especially in the years around 1885, when the Rijksmuseum moved to its current premises, several complete collections were bequeathed or donated to the museum. The collection of works by living masters – the 'modern art' of the period (displayed in Haarlem since 1838) – was also transferred to the Rijksmuseum at this point. In the same year the magnificent collection of paintings bequeathed to the city of Amsterdam in 1847 by Adriaan van der Hoop was likewise moved to the Rijksmuseum. This included such masterpieces as Rembrandt's *Jewish Bride* and Ruisdael's *Windmill at Wijk bij Duurstede.*

A major addition was Mr. and Mrs. Drucker-Fraser's collection, the various parts of which were donated or permanently lent to the museum from 1909 onwards, culminating in 1944 in a magnificent bequest comprising numerous works by artists of the Hague and Amsterdam schools. This collection, which includes *The Bridge over the Singel* by George Breitner, *The Truncated Mill* by Jacob Maris and *Morning Ride on the Beach* by Anton Mauve, forms the core of the museum's late nineteenth-century exhibits.

In 1908, with assistance from the Rembrandt Association, the museum succeeded in acquiring Johannes Vermeer's *Kitchen Maid,* while in 1921 *The Little Street,* also by Vermeer, was donated to the Rijksmuseum by Henri Deterding. Following the appointment of Frederick Schmidt-Degener as director in 1922, the museum underwent a major transformation. The idea that the entire collection should always be on display – which had led to complaints that the Rijksmuseum looked more like a warehouse than a museum – was now abandoned in favour of well-balanced exhibits in which every piece could be displayed to its full advantage. This has remained the museum's policy ever since. The most important donation in the period following the Second World War (during which much of the collection had been moved somewhere safer) was the bequest by Mr. and Mrs. De Bruijn-Van der Leeuw, including Jan Steen's *Woman at her Toilet* and Rembrandt's *Self-portrait as the Apostle Paul.* Without in any way underestimating the numerous valuable additions to the collection during the post-war years (often acquired with the help of the Rembrandt Association and the Rijksmuseum Foundation), the most important acquisition in the period leading up to the writing of this brief historical review was Rembrandt's *Portrait of Johannes Wtenbogaert* (1633), one of the great master's most striking early portraits.

Thus, over the years, the museum has succeeded in building up a fine and particularly representative collection of Dutch painting from the fifteenth to the turn of the twentieth century.

In addition to the collection described above, the museum also possesses a small collection of Southern Netherlandish, Italian and Spanish masters, including masterpieces by Peter Paul Rubens, Anthonie van Dijck (Anthony Vandyke), Lorenzo Monaco, Piero di Cosimo, Carlo Crivelli, Jacopo Tintoretto and Francisco de Goya. This collection, which does not constitute a representative selection of painting from countries outside the Netherlands, is not on permanent display.

Lorenzo Monaco (c 1372 - c 1424), *St. Jerome in his study*, c 1418, panel, 23 x 18 cm

St. Jerome, one of the Fathers of the Church, is depicted here as a scholar standing in his cell, surrounded by books. He can be identified by his attributes: the scarlet cardinal's hat at the side of the lectern, and the lion. The creature became St. Jerome's faithful companion after he had re- moved a thorn from its paw. Lorenzo refers to this legend by showing the lion raising its injured paw to the saint.

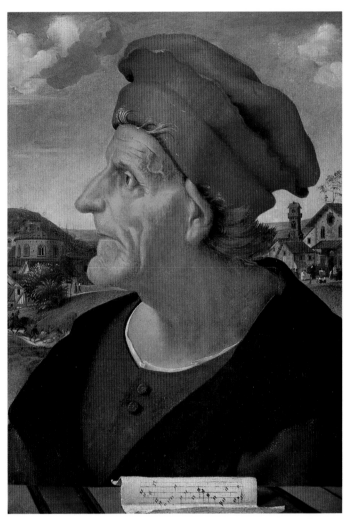

Carlo Crivelli (1435/1440 - after 1493), *Mary Magdalene*, c 1487, panel, 152 x 49 cm

According to hagiography, Mary Magdalene was a harlot who repented and became one of Jesus' most faithful followers. Artists generally depicted her wearing costly garments, with long blonde hair and holding a pot of ointment, because she had anointed the feet of Jesus. This is how Crivelli portrayed her, using a refined technique and subtle shades of colour. The panel is signed 'Opus Karoli Crivelli Venet', which means 'a work by Carlo Crivelli of Venice'.

Piero di Cosimo (1461/1462 - 1521), *Francesco Giamberti* and *Giuliano da Sangallo*, c 1482, panels, 47.5 x 33.5 cm

These portraits of father and son once formed a diptych. Francesco Giamberti was a carpenter employed by the Florentine De' Medici family. On occasion he also played music for them, hence the sheet music which appears in the portrait. His son Giuliano da Sangallo became an architect, which explains the compasses and the goose quill. When an old man he was even appointed architect of St. Peter's in Rome. The difference in age and status of the father and son is well rendered. Such meticulous realism is a typical feature of the Renaissance.

Northern Netherlandish, formerly attributed to **Geertgen tot Sint Jans** (1460/1465 - 1488/1493), *The adoration of the Magi*, c 1490, panel, 90 x 70 cm

The Magi are travelling to Bethlehem from three corners of the earth to worship the newborn infant Jesus. The painter shows this in the background. In the Middle Ages, the Magi were believed to have come from three different continents (Europe, Asia and Africa), hence their different-coloured skins. The figures are still somewhat stiff, but it is the realistic details that make the scene seem so genuine and appealing. Such attention to detail is characteristic of Dutch painting.

Jan Mostaert (c 1475 - 1555/1556), *The adoration of the Magi*, c 1510, panel, 49 x 35 cm

With a richly decorated gateway in the background, the Magi are offering gifts to the infant Jesus. Their cavalcades can be seen in the distance. Scarcely anything in this painting recalls Jesus' humble birth in a stable. The ox and the ass are tiny figures tucked away in a corner. The painting focuses entirely on Jesus in his mother's lap and on the gifts, in which he seems very interested. This playful element adds to the realism of the painting.

∧

Master of Alkmaar (active in first half of sixteenth century), *The seven works of charity*, 1504, panels, 101 x 54 cm

Feeding the hungry
Refreshing the thirsty
Clothing the naked
Burying the dead
Lodging the travellers
Visiting the sick
Comforting the captives

It is the Day of Judgment, and man is being judged by his good works. Christ is shown sitting in judgment on the midmost of the panels depicting the seven works of charity. These works are being performed by richly dressed men and women, in stark contrast to the group of beggars and cripples surrounding Christ. In the sixteenth century the panels were vandalized; the figures representing the rich and the clergy were the main targets.

∧
∧

Jacob Cornelisz van Oostsanen (before 1470 - 1533), *Saul and the Witch of Endor*, 1526, panel, 87.5 x 125 cm

According to the Book of Samuel, Saul visited a soothsayer on the eve of his battle with the Philistines. Invoking the spirit of Samuel, the woman predicted that Saul would lose the battle and be killed. Fascinated as he was by demons and witches, Jacob Cornelisz turned this biblical tale into a lively, fantastic witchcraft scene. Other episodes from the tale can be seen in the background.

∧

Jacob Cornelisz van Oostsanen (before 1470 - 1533), *Triptych showing the adoration of the Magi, donors and saints*, 1517, panel, centre panel 83 x 56 cm, wings 83 x 25 cm

This triptych depicts the adoration of the Magi, with the donors (an unknown couple and their children) portrayed on the side panels. In accordance with tradition the men are shown on the left, in this case together with their patron saint St. Jerome, and the women on the right with St. Catherine. The three-dimensional portrayal, involving the use of perspective, makes it seem as though the donors are witnessing the adoration.

^
^

Pieter Pietersz (1540/1541 - 1603), *Man and woman at a spinning wheel*, c 1570, panel, 76 x 63.5 cm

Jan van Scorel (1495 - 1562), *Mary Magdalene*, c 1528, panel, 67 x 76.5 cm

Jan Cornelisz Vermeyen (1500 - 1559), *The wedding in Cana*, c 1530, panel, 66 x 84.5 cm

This is not a portrait of a virtuous married couple, but a genre painting – an everyday scene with a hidden meaning. The man is trying to keep the woman from her work and is offering her a drink. She has not yet made up her mind and is still holding the reel and spindle. The message is clear: a virtuous woman should not let herself be led astray. This work by Pietersz – the son of Pieter Aertsen – is a forerunner of seventeenth-century genre painting.

The pot of ointment identifies this richly dressed woman as Mary Magdalene, who anointed the feet of Jesus. After Jesus' death she spent the rest of her life as a hermit, living in a cave. Angels transported her to heaven seven times a day. This story, which is taken from hagiography, is depicted in the background. Scorel was one of the first Dutch painters to travel to Italy and study Renaissance art, the influence of which can be seen in this painting.

The wedding is depicted in an unusual manner, showing the bride and groom, Mary, Jesus and the disciples at the wedding feast. This is based on an apocryphal bible story, in which the wedding in Cana is interpreted as the marriage of Jesus' disciple John to Mary Magdalene. In a fascinating nocturne, Vermeyen depicts the moment at which the bridegroom chooses a life with Jesus, rather than with his bride.

Pieter Aertsen (1509 - 1575), *The egg dance*, 1552, panel, 84 x 172 cm

Pieter Aertsen's peasant scenes are among the earliest examples of this genre in Dutch painting. One of the first is *The egg dance*. In this form of popular entertainment, the idea was to dance the egg into the chalk circle and then, only using one's feet, place the wooden bowl over it. This is an amusing scene full of erotic allusions, but the painting also contains a warning against such fool-ishness: one of the boards on the table shows a picture of a jester.

Lucas van Leyden (1494 - 1533), *Triptych with the adoration of the golden calf*, c 1530, panel, centre panel 93 x 67 cm, wings 91 x 30 cm

While Moses was on Mount Sinai receiving the Ten Commandments from God, the children of Israel rose up in revolt. Disobeying God's first commandment, they made a graven image of a golden calf and indulged in wild revelry. When Moses came down from the mountain, he saw what had happened and was filled with wrath. Lucas provides a highly realistic portrayal of these events in a landscape which is divided over the three panels. This painting helped pave the way for the Renaissance in the Netherlands.

The years around 1585 were a period of great uncertainty. The Dutch war of independence against the Spaniards was in full swing, and the Netherlands had become a Protestant country. Artists, who had been used to generous commissions from the Catholic Church, were no longer able to earn much.

Yet it was this period that saw the emergence of a spectacular artistic trend known as Dutch Mannerism. Subjects were borrowed from the Bible and the classics but depicted in an 'anti-classical' manner, with fi-gures - often nude - in unusual, contorted postures. This trend was derived from Prague Mannerism, which was known in the Netherlands through the engravings of Hendrick Goltzius, from works by Bartholomeus Spranger (a Prague-based Dutch artist who was the Mannerists' great model). Around 1600, artists began to turn away from the artifici-ality of Mannerism and allowed their compositions to become more restful. The famous engraver Hendrick Goltzius took up a new challenge and became a painter.

Karel van Mander (1548 - 1606), *The magnanimity of Scipio*, 1600, copper, 44 x 79 cm

When conquering Carthage, the Roman general Scipio had captured a young girl. Instead of keeping her for himself, Scipio displayed magnanimity by returning her to her fiancé and declaring that the ransom money should be her dowry. Karel van Mander painted this work on copper, on a white ground, which gives the colours great intensity.

Cornelis Cornelisz van Haarlem (1562 - 1638), *The massacre of the innocents*, 1590, canvas, 245 x 358 cm

When Jesus was born and King Herod heard that the infant was the King of the Jews, he ordered that all boy children in Bethlehem under two years of age should be put to death. Meanwhile, however, Mary and Joseph had fled to safety with their baby. The senseless slaughter of the innocents is an example of ruthless tyranny. The painting was probably commissioned on behalf of Prince Maurice, whose task as commander-in-chief of the army was to rid the Netherlands of Spanish tyranny.

Hendrick Goltzius (1558 - 1617), *Lot and his daughters*, 1616, canvas, 140 x 204 cm

After fleeing the sinful city of Sodom, which God had ordered to be destroyed, Lot and his daughters found themselves alone. Fearing that they would remain childless, the girls seduced their father into sleeping with them. This is shown on the left of the picture, while on the right in the background we can see Sodom burning. Goltzius gave a moralistic twist to this erotic bible story by including a fox as a symbol of cleverness and a dog as a guardian of morality.

Abraham Bloemaert (1564 - 1651), *The preaching of John the Baptist*, c 1600, canvas, 139 x 188 cm

In a highly varied landscape of farmsteads and oddly contorted tree-trunks, John the Baptist is preaching to a motley crowd. Bloemaert was not particularly concerned with the bible story, for he made John an inconspicuous figure, half-hidden in shadow beneath the tree. The artist was more interested in the figures, which he portrayed in unusual, often laboured poses. Such complication – which is also apparent in the landscape – is typical of Mannerism.

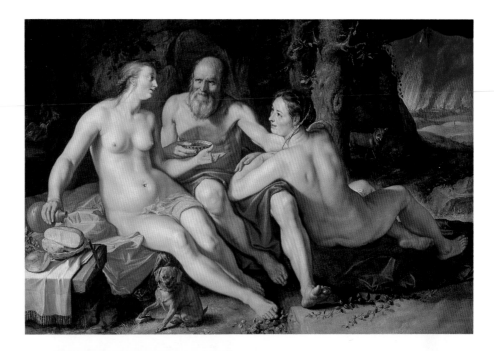

<

Cornelis Cornelisz van Haarlem (1562 - 1638), *The fall of man*, 1592, canvas, 273 x 220 cm

Adam and Eve are just about to commit the first sin, by eating of the only tree in the Garden of Eden whose fruit has been forbidden by God. This tree is pointed out to them in the background. But Adam and Eve also listened to the devil, who is offering them the fruit. This couple represents Cornelis van Haarlem's human ideal. The difference in colour emphasizes the difference between man and woman.

It was in the sixteenth century that the art of portraiture first developed in the Northern Netherlands. Portraits of nobility and clergy had been painted before then, but commoners had only had their portraits painted on altar-pieces, together with those of the saints after whom they were named. The first autonomous portraits of commoners - self-aware men, women and children - appeared around 1530. They were portrayed either alone, in couples or in groups. Married couples were not usually shown together, but separately, as counterparts. Attributes reveal how the subject wanted to be seen: as a merchant, a virtuous housewife or a pious Christian. Some painters painted portraits as a sideline, for example Maarten van Heemskerck, whose main work was historical paintings. Others specialized in portraiture. One of the first to do so was Dirck Jacobsz, the son of Jacob Cornelisz van Oostsanen. In 1529 he also painted the first portrait of a civic guard association, which was to become a Dutch speciality.

Maarten van Heemskerck (1498 - 1574), *Portrait of a woman, formerly identified as Anna Codde*, 1529, panel, 84.5 x 65 cm

The woman portrayed here is totally involved in her spinning, the typical occupation of a virtuous housewife. This depiction of activity, the foreshortening of arms and hands and the plastic rendering of the subject were all daring new features of Dutch portraiture around 1529. The inscription on the frame tells us that the woman was then 26 years old. Heemskerck, a pupil of Jan van Scorel's, painted her husband's portrait at the same time.

Dirck Jacobsz (1496 - 1567), *Pompeius Occo (1483 - 1537)*, 1531, panel, 66 x 54 cm

The escutcheon hanging from the branch tells us that this is Pompeius Occo: a man from East Friesland who had become an Amsterdam banker and merchant with international connections, a humanist and a prominent citizen, and also King Christian II of Denmark's diplomatic representative in the Netherlands. Jacobsz portrayed the banker as a self-assured individual. His attributes - a skull and a carnation - are references to Occo's religion, in which this earthly existence is merely transient but there is hope of eternal life. This picture of Occo is the first Renaissance portrait by an Amsterdam painter.

Anthonis Mor van Dashorst (1519 - 1575), *Sir Thomas Gresham (1519 - 1579)*, c 1565/1570, panel, 90 x 75.5 cm

From 1552 to 1567, the English merchant Thomas Gresham lived and worked in Antwerp as financial agent of the English crown ('King's merchant'). This prominent social position explains why he had his portrait painted by Mor, who was court artist to Philip II. This Utrecht-born painter was noted for the accurate recording of detail in his portraits. He depicted Gresham as a strong, somewhat reserved personality. Mor also painted a portrait of Gresham's wife, which is likewise in the Rijksmuseum.

The city of Utrecht had always had strong links with Rome, and many Utrecht artists went to Rome to study art and find work. When Hendrick ter Brugghen, Dirck van Baburen and Gerard van Honthorst were in Rome, from 1605 to 1620, they were particularly impressed by the paintings of Caravaggio (1573 - 1610). This Italian painter distinguished himself from his contemporaries by his realistic, natural approach to painting. He combined this with a dramatic treatment of light, involving sharp contrasts of light and shade. In particular, the simplicity, humanity and immediacy of Caravaggio's biblical scenes were the subject of much discussion. Although his rendering of ordinary or even ugly people was not much appreciated in Rome, it greatly appealed to the painters from Utrecht. They imitated Caravaggio in both style and choice of subjects, and in turn influenced Dutch painters such as Frans Hals and Rembrandt.

^
^

Gerard van Honthorst (1590 - 1656), *The merry fiddler*, 1623, canvas, 108 x 89 cm

^ ^

Hendrick ter Brugghen (1588 - 1629), *Heraclitus and Democritus*, 1628, canvas, 85.5 x 70 cm

This laughing fiddler, who is raising his glass to us so merrily from his window, was painted by Honthorst in 1623. The artist inscribed the year and his name on the window-sill. In this painting he imitated not only Caravaggio's style, but also his choice of subjects. Such semi-respectable figures – musicians, card-players and drinkers – in fanciful costumes were also painted by other Caravaggists.

Two Greek philosophers, each with a globe. On the left is Heraclitus as an old man, leaning on a globe of the earth and lamenting. He considered people so stupid that it made him weep, and we can see the tears running down his cheeks. Democritus is shown as a young man, leaning on a globe of the heavens and laughing at human stupidity. This theme of the weeping and the laughing philosopher was common among Dutch painters. The rugged heads and suntanned hands of Ter Brugghen's philosophers are typical of the Caravaggists.

Dirck van Baburen (c 1595 - 1624), *Prometheus being chained by Vulcan*, 1623, canvas, 202 x 184 cm

With Mercury looking on in amusement, Vulcan the god of fire is chaining Prometheus to a rock. The eagle which is to devour his liver every day – Prometheus' punishment for stealing fire from the gods and giving it to mankind – is hovering ominously in a corner. In this mythological scene, Van Baburen shows himself to be a true Caravaggist, with contrasts of light and shade, dramatic expressions and unidealized people with suntanned hands and faces.

Hendrick ter Brugghen (1588 - 1629), *The adoration of the Magi*, 1619, canvas, 134 x 160 cm

The wrinkled figure of Joseph, the equally wrinkled figure of the king bowing down, and the plump infant Jesus with his skin hanging in loose folds all make it clear that Ter Brugghen had no intention of idealizing his subjects' beauty. In other respects, however, this painting shows little of Caravaggio's influence – it is too static and colourful for that. In fact, it is the artist's use of colour that makes this painting so special, and gives the various fabrics such a convincing appearance.

After Mannerism, which in fact was mainly thought of as an international style, Northern Netherlandish painters began to search for new artistic possibilities and subjects from about 1600 onwards. They found them in their immediate environment: domestic interiors, the city, the sea and the countryside. This rapidly gave rise to a multitude of new genres that catered to the burghers' tastes, such as landscapes, seascapes and townscapes, still lifes, scenes from everyday life and architecture. Existing genres such as portraits and historical painting were given a new lease of life. Many painters concentrated on one particular subject. In fact, some were so specialized that they had to ask colleagues to paint parts of pictures which they themselves were not so good at. But there were also painters who were masters of several different genres, such as Rembrandt van Rijn.

Willem Buytewech (1591/1592 - 1624), *Dignified couples courting*, c 1617 - 1620, canvas, 56 x 70 cm

Here we see two elegantly dressed couples on a terrace by a fountain. A game is being played. The seated woman is holding a rosebud in each hand. The man at her side must choose one of the rosebuds without looking, thus choosing either the woman beside him or her companion. The woman has already made up her mind and has crossed her arms so that, whether the man answers 'left' or 'right', he is bound to choose her. Not without reason, Buytewech painted a spider's web behind the escutcheon hanging from the barred window.

Dirck Hals (1591 - 1656), *The fête champêtre*, 1627, panel, 78 x 137 cm

A party is taking place in idyllic parkland near a villa. The guests are wearing festive clothes and having a merry time eating, drinking, making music and flirting. Dirck Hals, a younger brother of Frans Hals, portrayed the various figures in great detail. He borrowed one or two of them – a woman and a dog – from Willem Buytewech. This outdoor party scene is not based on reality, but recalls the garden of love, a popular late medieval theme.

Adriaen Pietersz van de Venne (1589 - 1662), *The harbour of Middelburg*, 1625, panel, 64 x 134 cm

Van de Venne's picture of the harbour of Middelburg is an extremely lively one: ships with their flags hoisted, mounted horsemen, dogs, children, peasants, more horses, dignified figures in black, country estates – the list is almost endless. Van de Venne depicted all this in a wealth of anecdotic detail, with Middelburg outlined against the sky in the background.

Nicolaus Knüpfer (c 1603 - 1655), *Brothel scene, possibly an episode from a stage play*, c 1650, panel, 60 x 74.5 cm

Half-undressed, drunken males, bare-breasted females and a woman playing a stringed instrument – an exceptionally unbridled scene. The pair on the bed certainly appear to have lost all their inhibitions. Another couple is standing on the table. There can be no doubt that this is a brothel scene. Knüpfer, a German painter who settled in Utrecht, often borrowed subjects from the theatre.

Paulus Potter (1625 - 1654), *Two horses in a meadow by a hedge*, 1649, panel, 23.5 x 30 cm

Animals always feature prominently in Paulus Potter's paintings: horses, goats and above all cattle in a Dutch landscape. Here we see two horses which are viewed from a low angle and thus seem particularly striking. Each of the animals stands out against its background – the dark-brown horse against the cloudy sky, and the white horse against the group of trees. These contrasts, together with the stormy sky, create a sense of foreboding.

Jan Asselijn (after 1610 - 1652), *The threatened swan*, before 1652, canvas, 144 x 171 cm

Caesar van Everdingen (c 1617 - 1678), *Young woman as 'Winter'*, c 1650, canvas, 97 x 81 cm

With menacingly outspread wings, the swan is vigorously defending its nest against the dog swimming up from the left. The scattered feathers and the low angle from which the bird is viewed emphasize its fury. The painting includes a number of inscriptions: 'the Grand Pensionary' beneath the swan, 'Holland' on one of the eggs, and 'the enemy of the state' above the dog's head. These texts were added later, when the owner of the painting decided that the swan was meant to represent Grand Pensionary Johan de Witt, protecting Holland. In that case the enemy was presumably De Witt's adversary, England.

A young woman is warming her hands over a fire. Her hands are concealed under her skirt, which is spread over the pan of glowing embers. The girl represents Winter, a season which was usually depicted as an old man, symbolizing the closing phase of human life. With its meticulous detail and expert rendering of reflected light, Van Everdingen's 'Winter' is a fine example of the classical trend in seventeenth-century Dutch painting.

Pieter Saenredam (1597 - 1665), *Interior of the St. Odolphus church in Assendelft,* 1649, panel, 50 x 76 cm

'This is the church in Assendelft, a village in Holland, painted by Pieter Saenredam in the year 1649, on the 2nd of October.' The artist inscribed these words on the left-hand pew when the painting was finished. Church interiors were Saenredam's speciality. He was an extremely meticulous worker. First he made sketches, took measurements and prepared a mechanical drawing, using perspective. Only then did he make a start on the actual painting. The tombstone of Saenredam's father, who was buried in the St. Odolphus church, is shown in the foreground.

Gerrit Houckgeest (c 1600 - 1661), *Interior of the Oude Kerk in Delft,* 1654, panel, 49 x 41 cm

Illusionism is a important feature of church interiors as painted by Dutch artists. Houckgeest created this complex picture of the interior of the Oude Kerk (Old Church) by painting it from an unusual angle. The spatial illusion is heightened by the sunlight, and also by the curtain which Houckgeest painted in front of the interior. The curtain almost seems a genuine part of the scene – the curtain-rod has even cast its shadow on the arch. What this is, in effect, is a painting of a painting with a curtain in front of it.

Jan van de Cappelle (1626 - 1679), *The home fleet saluting the state barge,* 1650, panel, 64 x 92.5 cm

A large fleet is about to set sail. The leading vessel is firing the salute, which is being answered by the ship on the right. In the centre we can see the state barge, full of high government officials. Van de Cappelle used a combination of silver-grey and orange tones in depicting this scene. He was not concerned with recording a specific event, but wanted to convey an impression of ships, clouds, fire and smoke and their reflections in the smooth water.

Adriaen van Ostade (1610 - 1685), *Peasants in an interior,* also known as *The skaters,* 1650, panel, 44 x 35.5 cm

In a shadowy inn, some peasants are sitting together by the hearth. It must be freezing outside, for there is a pair of skates on the floor. The atmosphere inside the inn is warm and cheerful. People are chatting and smoking, and there is a pewter jug of wine. In those days smoking was considered a despicable habit, mainly indulged in by the common people. Adriaen van Ostade specialized in depictions of peasant life, and frequently painted tavern scenes of this kind.

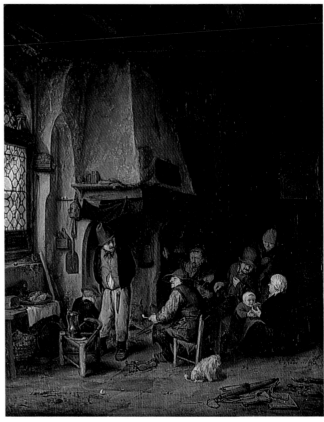

In the opening years of the seventeenth century, artists in Haarlem started to discover their immediate environment - the Dutch landscape with its farmsteads and trees, its windmills and panoramas. The countryside was no longer simply a source of inspiration for pastoral fantasies, as had been customary up to then. Artists gradually broke away from the Flemish manner of landscape painting. Horizons became lower, and the contrast in colour between foreground and background grew less pronounced. The now familiar features of Dutch landscape paintings - broad and flat, with great emphasis on water and sky - became established. A number of specialities developed within landscape painting: river scenes, winter scenes, panoramas, dunes and woodlands. Some artists preferred to paint idealized Italian landscapes rather than their own surroundings. These artists were referred to as Italianates.

Hendrick Avercamp (1585 - 1634), *Winter landscape with ice skaters*, c 1608, panel, 77.5 x 132 cm

Hercules Segers (1589/1590 - in or before 1638), *River valley*, c 1625, panel, 30 x 53.5 cm

An endless expanse of ice, a wintry atmosphere and a huge crowd of people - all typical ingredients of Avercamp's countless winter scenes. With its elevated horizon, this early work is still reminiscent of paintings by the Flemish artist Pieter Bruegel. Avercamp portrayed his dozens of different figures in great detail - skating, losing their balance, riding in sleighs or chatting together. Others are shown going about their daily business. Avercamp inscribed his name on the small shed to the right.

The composition of this fanciful landscape by Segers recalls the work of Flemish painters, with dark colours in the foreground and bluish-grey in the distance. Yet, with its broad horizon, this is a deeper panorama than De Momper's. It is also less artificial: it seems like a real landscape, wild and inhospitable. The solitary walkers accentuate this sense of desolation. Segers painted only a few landscapes, all of them highly original, and characterized by visible brushwork and a limited range of colours.

Joos de Momper (1564 - 1635), *River landscape with wild boar hunt*, c 1610, panel, 121 x 196.5 cm

Amid steep cliffs and mighty castles, an almost endless vista: a river full of boats and ships, an island with a castle on it and a small town on the shore. The cliffs are connected by a bridge, there are glimpses into the depths of a forest, and a wild boar hunt is going on. This painting by De Momper is a fanciful landscape in the Flemish tradition. The artist's elevated viewpoint and his use of vistas and colour contrasts serve to create an illusion of depth.

Salomon van Ruysdael (1600/1603 - 1670), *River landscape with ferry*, 1649, canvas, 99.5 x 133.5 cm

Salomon van Ruysdael was an uncle of Jacob van Ruisdael's (who spelt his name with an 'i' rather than a 'y'). Unlike those of his famous nephew, Salomon's landscapes emanate peace and tranquillity. This river scene is a good example, despite the clouds scudding across the sky (which the painter emphasized by lowering the horizon even more than usual). Like Esaias van de Velde, Ruysdael chose as his subject a typically Dutch scene with a ferry as its central feature.

Esaias van de Velde (1587 - 1630), *The ferry*, 1622,
panel, 75.5 cm x 113 cm

A truly Dutch landscape, with its low horizon,
cloudy skies and a winding river with windmills,
trees and boats reflected in it. In the foreground
we see a ferry transporting passengers, a horse
and cart and some cows. This work by Van de
Velde is an early milestone in Dutch landscape
painting. Despite being painted in a studio, rather
than directly from nature, it is a convincingly portrayed, familiar landscape.

Jan van Goyen (1596 - 1656), *Landscape with two oaks*,
1641, canvas, 88.5 x 110.5 cm

A pair of ancient oaks stand out against a grey sky.
Two men are resting beneath the trees. The panorama to the left shows a town by a river, towards
which a third figure is heading. This is a simple
composition with a low horizon, executed in
various shades of grey, green, yellow and brown.
The only touch of real colour is the man's red
jacket. Van Goyen's main concern here was how
to convey space and atmosphere.

Philips Koninck (1619-1688), *Distant view with cottages lining a road*, c 1655, canvas, 133 x 167.5 cm

Philips Koninck, a pupil of Rembrandt's, specialized in extensive panoramas. His subject was the river landscape of Gelderland, which he painted again and again, using a simple range of colours and visible brushwork. This particular panorama is completely unbroken, and the blurred horizon makes it seem even more immense. The effect is further enhanced by the alternation of light and shade. Although it appears genuine, Koninck's landscape does not seem to be identifiable.

Aert van der Neer (1603/1604 - 1677), *River scene in winter*, c 1655-60, canvas, 64 x 79 cm

A frozen river stretches away to a blurred, distant horizon. To the left we can see the houses and steeples of a town, to the right the countryside. As in Avercamp's paintings, the ice is full of people skating, sledging and playing 'kolfspel' (seemingly an early form of golf). But the atmosphere in Van der Neer's winter scene is different – less cheerful and colourful. This is mainly because of the low horizon and the wintry sky reflected in the icy river.

Jacob van Ruisdael (1628/1629 - 1682), *The windmill at Wijk bij Duurstede*, c 1670, canvas, 83 x 101 cm

A stone windmill, viewed from a low angle, stands out against a sky full of dark clouds. Water and land are lit up by occasional patches of sunlight breaking through the clouds. In this painting Ruisdael turned an ordinary Dutch river scene into an outstanding work of art. The river is the Lek, and the town is Wijk bij Duurstede in the province of Utrecht. In Ruisdael's work, seventeenth-century Dutch landscape painting reached a pinnacle.

Meindert Hobbema (1638 - 1709), *The watermill*,
c 1665, panel, 62 x 85.5 cm

Hobbema's paintings very much recall the work
of Jacob van Ruisdael, of whom he is the only
known pupil. He shared Ruisdael's preference for
wooded landscapes, water and watermills. However, unlike Ruisdael's landscapes, Hobbema's are
not dramatic, but instead more cheerful, lighter
in colour and above all livelier. Watermills are a
favourite subject of Hobbema's, featuring in at
least forty of his paintings.

Jacob van Ruisdael (1628/1629 - 1682), *View of
Haarlem*, c 1670, canvas, 43 x 38 cm

This small painting is one of a series of panoramas showing the skyline of Haarlem, and therefore known as haarlempjes ('little Haarlems').
This particular work is a view of Haarlem from
the dunes at Overveen, where we can see linen
being bleached at the local laundries. Unlike
Koninck, Ruisdael chose a vertical layout for his
panorama, with an extremely low horizon. This
allowed him to devote three-quarters of his canvas to the cloudy sky. Although the sky is somewhat gloomy, the sun is breaking through gaps in
the clouds and lighting up parts of the landscape.

^

Jan Both (c 1615 - 1652), *Italian landscape with man drawing*, c 1650, canvas, 187 x 240 cm

A party of travellers is resting by a mountain stream. One of them is drawing, while another is looking over his shoulder. Nearby we can see a herd of goats. To the right is a panorama of sunlit mountains. Jan Both frequently painted landscapes with groups of travellers, with particular emphasis on scenery. He was an Italianate, one of a group of artists who specialized in painting Italian landscapes bathed in warm, golden light.

<

Adam Pijnacker (c 1620 - 1673), *Boatmen moored on the shore of an Italian lake*, 1668, canvas on panel, 97.5 x 85.5 cm

Boats are moored on the shore of a lake surrounded by high mountains. The countryside is set aglow by golden light which picks out features such as the white bark of the birch-tree, the woman and child, and the ox and the ass. The presence of these animals may indicate that the painting is meant to represent Mary's flight to Egypt with the infant Jesus, but this is uncertain. Pijnacker was one of the Italianates.

Aelbert Cuyp (1620 - 1691), *River landscape with horsemen*, c 1655, canvas, 128 x 227.5 cm

Although clearly influenced by Italianates such as Jan Both, Aelbert Cuyp never went to Italy. Cuyp spent all his life in Dordrecht and only painted Dutch landscapes, bathed in Mediterranean light. The inspiration for this hilly landscape with cattle and horsemen came from a sketch which Cuyp made during a visit to the Wijlermeer area (between Nijmegen and Kleve) in 1651 - 1652. He achieved the golden glow so beloved of the Italianates by painting the scene in the late afternoon sun, with elongated shadows.

Willem Claesz Heda (1594/1595 - c 1680), *Still life with gilt goblet*, 1635, panel, 88 x 113 cm

At first sight, these are simply the remains of a sumptuous meal: half-empty glasses, an upset drinking-vessel, some pieces of bread, oyster shells, crumpled napkins and a cut lemon. Yet Heda deliberately selected and arranged the precious items so to display his technique to the best advantage. His rendering of light reflecting off the various materials – silver, silver-gilt, pewter and glass – is masterly. This monochrome painting is a high point in the work of Heda, who is known to have produced some 70 still lifes.

Hans Bollongier (c 1600 - after 1645), *Still life with flowers*, 1639, panel, 68 x 54.5 cm

However ordinary this bouquet of tulips, roses, anemones, carnations and the occasional primula may at first appear, those who are familiar with symbols of human transience can again find them here. The creatures on the table are there to remind us that flowers do not last. Of all the flowers here, the tulip is particularly apt as a symbol of transience. When tulip bulbs were first introduced into the Netherlands at the end of the sixteenth century, they became popular collectors' items, and in the 1630s they were bought and sold for astronomical sums – until 1637, when the market abruptly collapsed.

Abraham van Beyeren (1620/1621 - 1690), *Still life*, c 1665, canvas, 126 x 106 cm

Van Beyeren's still lifes are usually full of splendid silverware, glassware, china and luscious fruit. This painting, which contains all kinds of precious objects and delicacies, is no exception. Yet lurking among all this are a pocket-watch and some wilting roses, symbolizing the transience of earthly possessions. A constantly recurring feature of Van Beyeren's paintings is the reflection of the artist's studio in the gold and silver objects.

Jan de Bray (1627 - 1697), *The Haarlem printer Abraham Casteleyn and his wife Margarieta van Bancken*, 1663, canvas, 84 x 108 cm

Casteleyn and his wife had their portrait painted with their hands joined, as a sign of marital fidelity. Being Mennonites, they are soberly dressed, without any trace of finery. The couple are shown sitting on a terrace surrounded by books, a globe and a bust of Laurens Janszoon Coster, who people in Haarlem claimed had invented printing. These objects were not chosen at random, but were references to Casteleyn's profession. He was a printer and founder of the *Haerlemsche Courant*, one of the leading newspapers of the day.

<

Bartholomeus van der Helst (1613 - 1670), *Princess Henrietta Maria Stuart (1631 - 1660)*, 1652, canvas, 199.5 x 170 cm

When Van der Helst painted this portrait of Princess Mary of England, she was 21 years old and a widow, her husband William II, Prince of Orange (1626 – 1650), having died two years earlier. She is shown here in white mourning dress, seated beneath the Stadholders' Gate at the Binnenhof in The Hague. In her hand she is holding an orange, symbolizing the House of Orange. For the Amsterdam artist Van der Helst, painting the princess's portrait must have been a prestigious assignment.

Gerard ter Borch (1617 - 1681), *Helena van der Schalke (1646 - 1671)*, c 1648, panel, 34 x 28.5 cm

When Gerard ter Borch painted this portrait of Reverend van der Schalke's daughter, she was about two years old. She is wearing her prettiest dress, trimmed with ribbons and lace, and a large gold chain. We can just see part of the leading reins which Helena's mother must have used to restrain her. But here no-one is restraining her; she is all alone in a large empty room, looking slightly bewildered, with big dark eyes staring from her thin little face.

Together with Rembrandt and Vermeer, Frans Hals is considered one of the great seventeenth-century Dutch painters. Shortly after he was born (in Antwerp), his family moved to Haarlem, where Frans developed into a master portrait painter. He also produced genre paintings, some of which very much resemble portraits.

Hals' portraits are notable for their fluent style and bright colours, the unusual attitudes and gestures of the subjects, and the lively, often cheerful expressions on their faces. These are real, flesh-and-blood individuals. Although most of Hals' portraits were commissioned by well-to-do citizens, government officials and civic guard associations in Haarlem, he also received occasional commissions from Amsterdam.

Frans Hals (1582/1583 - 1666), *The merry drinker*, 1628/1630, canvas, 81 x 66.5 cm

Frans Hals used rapid, loose brushwork to portray this lively character. The brushstrokes range from the broad and vigorous to the brief and rhythmical. The artist's use of colour is limited: yellow, white, black and the odd touch of red. Nowhere do we find elaborate detail; instead, shapes are suggested with a few well-chosen brushstrokes. The glass, for example, consists of just a few lines, with the odd dab of white paint to suggest reflected light. It is not known whether this is a portrait or simply someone chosen at random.

Frans Hals (1582/1583 - 1666), *Wedding portrait of Isaac Abrahamsz Massa and Beatrix van der Laen, married in Haarlem on the 25th of April 1622*, c 1622, canvas, 140 x 166.5 cm

An informal portrait of a wealthy merchant and a burgomaster's daughter, Isaac Massa and Beatrix van der Laen, sitting in a garden. The portrait was painted shortly after they had got married. Various references to love and fidelity make it clear that this is a wedding portrait. The ivy and the vine around the tree are both symbols of steadfast love, while the thistle at the husband's side represents male fidelity. What makes this portrait so remarkable is the couple's relaxed pose.

Frans Hals (1582/1583 - 1666), *Portrait of a man, possibly Nicolaes Hasselaer*, 1630/1635, canvas, 79.5 x 66.5 cm

A distinguished citizen, fashionably dressed, with a large lace collar and a walking-stick in his hand. Hals portrayed the man in an unusual attitude, half-turning in his chair, with one arm over the seat-back. This gives the portrait an informal quality. It is as though the painter had asked his subject to look round for a moment, as in a snapshot. The man may be Nicolaes Hasselaer, an Amsterdam patrician.

Rembrandt was born in Leiden on 15 July 1606, the son of the miller Harmen Gerritsz van Rijn. At first he was apprenticed to painters in Leiden, but later he was taught by Pieter Lastman of Amsterdam. On 22 June 1634 Rembrandt married Saskia van Uylenburgh. Their son Titus was born in 1641; Saskia died a year later. In 1649, following Geertje Dircx, Hendrickje Stoffels became Rembrandt's housekeeper and mistress. In 1656 Rembrandt went bankrupt. He died in 1669 and was buried in the Westerkerk in Amsterdam.

Rembrandt was an inventive artist, unequalled in the depiction of ideas. He was mainly a historical painter, painting scenes from the bible, mythology and classical history. He also earned plenty of money painting portraits. In addition to this, he painted landscapes and the occasional still life.

Rembrandt van Rijn (1606 - 1669), *Tobias and Anna with the kid*, 1626, panel, 39.5 x 30 cm

Tobias was a wealthy, God-fearing man. His faith in God was put to the test when he became blind and went bankrupt. One day, when his wife Anna came home with a young goat, Tobias thought she had stolen it. Anna was furious that Tobias should suspect her of such a thing. This dramatic moment is depicted here by Rembrandt. Anna is wide-eyed with astonishment, but Tobias has already repented and is praying to God. This is one of Rembrandt's earliest works.

Rembrandt van Rijn (1606 - 1669), *Self-portrait as a young man*, 1628, panel, 22.6 x 18.7 cm

Rembrandt was twenty-two years old when he painted this self-portrait. What is remarkable about it is that the face is almost invisible, being largely hidden in shadow. Only Rembrandt's cheek and part of his ear are illuminated. Rembrandt probably painted this portrait as a study, in order to experiment with light and shade. He accentuated the hair by making scratches in the paint while it was still wet.

Rembrandt van Rijn (1606 - 1669), *Jeremiah lamenting the destruction of Jerusalem*, 1630, panel, 58 x 46 cm

Rembrandt depicted the old prophet in meticulous detail, with a wrinkled forehead and fluffy white beard. In contrast, the surroundings are blurred: Jeremiah is shown in an obscure setting, at the foot of two pillars. Away to the left we can see Jerusalem blazing, and King Nebuchadnezzar's troops entering the city. The prophet Jeremiah had foretold the destruction of Jerusalem, but the city could no longer be saved.

Rembrandt van Rijn (1606 - 1669), *Portrait of Johannes Wtenbogaert*, 1633, canvas, 130 x 103 cm

A lively portrait of one of the main religious leaders of Rembrandt's day, the preacher Johannes Wtenbogaert. Wtenbogaert (1557 – 1644) was the leader of the Remonstrants, and played an important part in their theological conflict with the Gomarists (a strict Calvinistic group). The young artist produced an impressive portrait of the old man, emphasizing Wtenbogaert's wrinkled features and the white, almost transparent linen collar underneath.

Rembrandt van Rijn (1606 - 1669), *The prophetess Anna*, 1631, panel, 60 x 48 cm

Light is shining from behind the aged prophetess, illuminating her gilt bonnet and red velvet mantle and giving the edges a silvery sheen. Anna was a prophetess who spent her days and nights praying in the temple, and recognized the infant Jesus as the Messiah. Rembrandt's mother may well have served as a model for this painting. In 1631, when Rembrandt produced this work, she was 60 years old.

Rembrandt van Rijn (1606 - 1669), *Landscape with stone bridge*, c 1638, panel, 29.5 x 42.5 cm

In the course of his career, Rembrandt drew and etched a good many landscapes, but only painted a few. What is unusual about this Dutch landscape is the menacing storm and the dramatic light. This is not an existing landscape, although Rembrandt presumably drew his inspiration for this painting from the countryside round Amsterdam.

Rembrandt van Rijn (1606 - 1669), *Portrait of Maria Trip*, 1639, panel, 107 x 82 cm

This finely dressed lady was twenty years old when Rembrandt painted her portrait. Her name was Maria Trip, and she was the daughter of a wealthy Amsterdam merchant. Rembrandt made use of her sumptuous clothing to achieve a striking interplay of light and shade. Her collar is made up of several layers of lace, while her waist and the front of her dress are decorated with costly gold lace. In her hand she is holding a fan with a ribbon attached to it.

Rembrandt van Rijn (1606 - 1669), *The Syndics of the Drapers' Guild*, 1662, canvas, 191.5 x 279 cm

Rembrandt van Rijn (1606 - 1669), *Self-portrait as the apostle Paul*, 1661, canvas, 91 x 77 cm

When he was 56, Rembrandt painted this impressive portrait of five inspectors of the cloth which was traded in Amsterdam. These men, known as the Syndics, are glancing up as though they have been interrupted in the course of their work. This painting also shows the Syndics' servant (the man without a hat). Rembrandt made allowances for the fact that the painting would be hung high up on the wall of the Drapers' Guildhall. He adjusted the perspective of the table to make it seem as though it was being viewed from slightly underneath.

Here Rembrandt portrayed himself as the apostle Paul. He is holding a bundle of letters – the epistles which St. Paul wrote to the Christian communities of Asia Minor. St. Paul ultimately paid for his Christian faith with his life, by being decapitated, and a sword has been his attribute ever since. In this painting, the hilt of the sword can be seen protruding from his coat. The light is shining down from the top left-hand corner, illuminating the turban and Rembrandt's features. Rembrandt was 55 years old at the time.

Rembrandt van Rijn (1606 - 1669), *The Jewish Bride*, 1667, canvas, 121.5 x 166.5 cm

Although this painting became known as *The Jewish Bride* in the nineteenth century, it is by no means certain that the woman in question actually was a Jewish bride. The couple may be contemporaries of Rembrandt's who had themselves portrayed as the biblical characters Isaac and Rebecca. In this work, Rembrandt used a variety of painting techniques. The faces and hands are relatively smooth, whereas the paint on the man's sleeve is very thick, indicating that Rembrandt applied it with a palette knife. He thus used the paint to convey not only colour, but also relief.

Rembrandt van Rijn (1606 - 1669), *Titus as a monk*, 1660, canvas, 79.5 x 67.5 cm

Rembrandt painted this portrait of his son Titus in 1660, when the lad was 19 years old. Titus is shown wearing the brown habit of a Capuchin monk. Rembrandt may have meant this to represent St. Francis of Assisi, using his son as a model. Titus often served as a model for historical, biblical or mythological characters. To Rembrandt, the monk's habit was also a technical challenge; he skilfully rendered the thick woollen material in various shades of brown.

In the seventeenth century, civic guard associations were always involved in major celebrations and whenever important visitors came to the city. The civic guard had traditionally been responsible for defending the city, but by the Golden Age the civic guard associations had simply become banqueting and drinking clubs for gentlemen of substance.

These associations, which regularly commissioned group portraits, were among painters' most important patrons. Portraits were sometimes commissioned to mark special occasions, such as a new captainship or colonelcy, or the inauguration of a new banquet hall. The portraits were used to decorate the association buildings, traditionally known as doelen ('shooting-ranges'). When inaugurating a new hall at the Kloveniersdoelen in Amsterdam, the association decided to commission six group portraits, one of which was painted by Rembrandt. In this painting, which was destined to become world-famous as *The Night Watch*, Rembrandt created an exceptional work of art.

Rembrandt van Rijn (1606 - 1669), *The company of Captain Frans Banning Cocq and Lieutenant Willem van Ruytenburch*, also known as *The Night Watch*, 1642, canvas, 363 x 437 cm

A company of the Amsterdam civic guard is preparing to march. The captain, dressed in black, is issuing a command: his arm is outstretched, the heel of his left foot is slightly raised, and his mouth is open. Instead of arranging the guardsmen in a neat row, as was the custom at the time, Rembrandt painted them exactly as they appeared at a given moment. The result is an unconstrained portrayal of the civic guard in action. The effect is enhanced by the artist's dramatic use of light.

Throughout his career Rembrandt had a large number of pupils and assistants. His studio mainly attracted painters who had learnt their craft elsewhere and now wanted to adopt Rembrandt's style.

Rembrandt's assistants contributed to the output of the studio. In fact, some pupils succeeded in imitating the master's style so well that it became hard to tell the difference between their work and a genuine Rembrandt. This led to the misconception that anything looking like a Rembrandt must actually be one.

Since 1967, a group of experts has been examining every painting attributed to Rembrandt. This examination has produced surprising results. While the number of 'official' Rembrandts is diminishing, the number of paintings attributed to famous pupils such as Dou, Flinck and Maes is still growing.

Gerard Dou (1613 - 1675), *Old woman reading a lectionary*, c 1630, panel, 71 x 55.5 cm

Typical of Dou is his meticulous rendering of all kinds of materials, be it fur, cloth, printed paper or an elderly woman's wrinkled skin. Perfect imitation is his main concern. Dou began as a pupil of Rembrandt's when the master was still young. While Rembrandt himself branched off in a different direction, Dou continued painting in Rembrandt's early manner. Dou became the father of 'precision' painting. His works were held in great esteem in his own day, and he became a model for countless pupils and imitators.

Govert Flinck (1615 - 1660), *Isaac blessing Jacob*, 1638, canvas, 117 x 141 cm

Sightless Isaac is raising his hand to give his blessing. With the other hand he is feeling Jacob's hand, which is covered with goatskin to make him seem as hairy as his older twin brother, Esau. The tension can be seen on Jacob's and Rebecca's faces. Isaac falls for the trick and blesses Jacob instead of Esau. Flinck painted this biblical story three years after leaving Rembrandt's studio. Rembrandt's influence is very apparent.

Nicolaes Maes (1634 - 1693), *Old woman at prayer*, also known as *The never-ending prayer*, canvas, 134 x 113 cm

Deep, glossy black and warm red are frequently occurring colours in Nicolaes Maes' work. Maes always painted with great attention to detail. Here the various materials are rendered with lifelike accuracy: the bread-crust, the pink slices of salmon laid out on the pewter dish, the stone tankard, the brown porringer. With the old woman rapt in prayer, the cat is trying to steal some food off the table.

Genre paintings are paintings which depict people going about their daily business in and around the home, at work or in the tavern. Although such paintings seem like snapshots, copied directly from real life, in actual fact they were created in the artist's studio. Often – but not always! – such seemingly lifelike genre paintings conceal a message which we in the twentieth century may no longer readily perceive. In the seventeenth century, on the other hand, paintings were supposed to educate or entertain. Sometimes the message is still very obvious, but sometimes an effort must be made to decipher it. In other cases, however, these domestic scenes were quite simply meant as decoration for the wall.

Gerard ter Borch (1617 - 1681), *Gallant conversation*, also known as *The paternal admonition*, c 1654, canvas, 71 x 73 cm

Although this painting was once known as *The paternal admonition*, this is certainly not a father admonishing his daughter in her bedchamber. The finely dressed woman is in fact a prostitute, the man (who is a soldier) is her client, and the woman sipping from a glass is the procuress. Other indicators that this is a brothel scene are the large red four-poster bed and also the dog and the candle, which symbolize lust.

Pieter de Hooch (1629 - after 1683), *Interior with women beside a linen chest*, 1663, canvas, 72 x 77.5 cm

The maidservant is holding a pile of clean laundry for the lady of the house, who is putting it away in the cupboard. On the right is a little boy playing with a 'kolf' stick (used for a game somewhat resembling golf). The scene is the canal-side residence of a well-to-do Amsterdam family. Through the open door we can glimpse the canal and even the houses on the other side – a typical feature of paintings by Pieter de Hooch.

Gabriël Metsu (1629 - 1667), *The sick child*, canvas, 32.2 x 27.2 cm

The sick child droops listlessly on the woman's lap. On top of the cabinet we see a porringer – the woman is trying to feed the child. The woman may represent the figure of Caritas, i.e. Christian charity. Metsu produced an attractive rendering of this domestic scene, using mostly browns and greys in the top left-hand corner of the painting and bright red, blue, yellow and green in the bottom right-hand corner. Such portrayals of sick children are extremely rare in the seventeenth century.

Jan Steen is known above all for his paintings of everyday scenes - merry gatherings, families round a table, taverns full of customers and so on. He was a fine raconteur and always a moralist. Almost every one of Steen's paintings contains a moral. His pictures are often exuberant, full of noise and disorder (to this day an untidy, lively household is referred to in Dutch as a 'Jan Steen household').

Steen was skilled at rendering various emotional expressions. He was also an expert painter of such different materials as glass, copper dishes, satin fabrics and fur. And he had a good eye for detail, such as the folds in a tablecloth or the reflection of light on crockery and glass. Jan Steen was a prolific artist - he is known to have produced some 400 paintings.

Jan Havicksz Steen (1626 - 1679), *The feast of St. Nicholas*, canvas, 82 x 70 cm

It is December the 5th - the eve of St. Nicholas' day - and the family have gathered to celebrate. The children have just received their presents, except for the boy on the left, who is crying because his shoe contains nothing but a switch (traditionally given to naughty children). His younger brother is pointing to the shoe and the switch and making fun of him. But, in the background, grandmother can be seen beckoning to the weeping boy - perhaps she has a parcel for him behind the curtain. The lozenge-shaped cake in the foreground on the right, known as a 'duivekater', was eaten on festive occasions.

Jan Havicksz Steen (1626 - 1679), *Woman at her toilet*, panel, 37 x 27.5 cm

A young woman is sitting on the edge of her bed, taking off a red stocking. The marks of the garters can still be seen on her legs. In the seventeenth century, women who wore red stockings were usually prostitutes. Another pointer in this direction is the half-full chamber pot on the floor: in those days the term *piskous* - 'piddle-stocking' - was used in Dutch to refer to a whore. Other symbols of lust in this context are the slippers which the woman has kicked off, the dog, and the candlestick on the chair.

Jan Havicksz Steen (1626 - 1679), *The merry family*, 1668, canvas, 110.5 x 141 cm

The family in this sitting-room are having a jolly time laughing, drinking, singing, smoking and making music. But the painter did not merely want to depict a family in high spirits. This is made clear by the sheet of paper on the mantelpiece, on which we can see the words of a Dutch proverb: 'The young ones chirrup as the old ones used to sing', meaning that the young tend to imitate their elders.

Jan Havicksz Steen (1626 - 1679), *The sick woman*, canvas, 76 x 63.5 cm

The doctor is feeling a sick young woman's pulse. What can she be suffering from? In fact, nothing much. Probably she is hopelessly smitten with the pangs of love. Steen's contemporaries could immediately tell that this was not a genuine visit by a real doctor. His clothing, which was very old-fashioned even in Steen's day, was the kind worn by doctors in stage plays. So Steen's 'doctor' was a caricature.

There are only about thirty known paintings by the Delft artist Johannes Vermeer: two historical paintings, a view of Delft, a little street and a series of interiors. Like his fellow artists from Delft, Vermeer was fascinated by space and the play of light on surfaces. The illusionistic interiors of Pieter de Hooch (1629 - after 1683), who settled in Delft around 1652, must have made an especially strong impression on Vermeer, for around 1658 he too began to devote himself to this particular genre. Unlike De Hooch, however, he concentrated on a single figure in a corner of a room, standing by a window with sunlight entering through it. The light played over the figure and the objects in the room, thereby giving it shape. Vermeer was a careful worker, with an eye for the tiniest details. Yet often it seems as though he has caught his subjects in the middle of some activity such as reading a letter, or pouring out milk. The effect is almost photographic.

Johannes Vermeer (1632 - 1675), *View of houses in Delft*, also known as *The Little Street*, c 1658, canvas, 54.3 x 44 cm

The houses in this painting look as genuine as if Vermeer had painted them from a window in his own house. And yet he did not; the picture is probably a fantasy, although one based on reality. Like De Hooch, Vermeer used illusionistic glimpses through doorways to suggest depth. But Vermeer achieved a far more convincing result, so much so that in the nineteenth century the painting was described as 'a photograph that has come alive'.

Johannes Vermeer (1632 - 1675), *The kitchen maid*,
c 1660, canvas, 45.5 x 41 cm

The woman is pouring milk out of a jug with the
utmost concentration. There is hardly any action
in this painting – the only movement seems to be
the trickle of milk. What is fascinating is the light,
which gives shape to the figure of the woman and
the various objects. Tiny dots of paint suggest
light reflecting off the loaf and the basket. Every
detail has been carefully worked out. This can be
seen particularly clearly in the depiction of the
wall, with nail-holes and even a nail casting a
shadow.

Johannes Vermeer (1632 - 1675), *Woman reading a letter*, 1662/1663, canvas, 46.5 x 39 cm

Here again, the painting focuses on a single character: a woman who is intently reading a letter. She is standing by a table with chairs round it, and there is a large map of Holland on the wall. Her face is turned to the light entering through an imaginary window. The composition is reduced to the bare minimum, as is the range of colours (mainly blue and yellow). Vermeer created a masterpiece out of very few resources.

Johannes Vermeer (1632 - 1675), *The love letter*,
1669/1670, canvas, 44 x 38.5 cm

Sitting in a Dutch interior is a well-to-do lady with
a letter in her hand. She has just stopped playing
her lute and is gazing expectantly at her maidservant. What could be in the letter? The answer to
this question may be concealed in the paintings
on the wall – a seascape and a landscape. In those
days the sea was sometimes compared to love with
its recurring storms, and a lover to a ship which
stayed in port only briefly. The walker in the
landscape painting appears to be departing. The
point of view chosen by the artist – looking
through a doorway – increases the photographic
effect.

Melchior d'Hondecoeter (1636 - 1695), *Pelican and other birds near a pool,* also known as *The floating feather,* c 1680, canvas, 159 x 144 cm

This painting of miscellaneous birds was commissioned from Melchior d'Hondecoeter by Stadholder William III for his hunting lodge known as Soestdijk (now a royal palace). Among wealthy owners of country estates it was the fashion to keep exotic species of birds and animals in a menagerie. Like unusual plants, these rare creatures were recorded for posterity by artists. D'Hondecoeter specialized in paintings of fowl.

Willem van de Velde II (1633 - 1707), *A ship on the high seas caught by a squall,* also known as *The gust,* c 1680, canvas, 77 x 63.5 cm

Of Dutch seascape painters, Willem van de Velde the Elder (1611 - 1693) and the Younger are the best known. They painted not just ships, but ships in action, in outstanding technical detail, and served in naval battles as 'reporters'. From 1672, father and son were employed by the English crown. This painting of two ships in distress amid raging seas – a stirring scene in which both vessels and elements are depicted with great technical skill – originates from that period.

Attributed to **Alejandro de Loarte** (died in 1626), *Kitchen scene*, c 1625, canvas, 100 x 122 cm

A man holds out a bowl invitingly. He is standing behind a table with meat and fish displayed on it. The whole scene is carefully composed and symmetrically constructed, with the various items barely overlapping. The artist depicted them in extremely lifelike detail: the pigeon hanging next to the sea bream, the quails on the left and the turkey's head on the right. De Loarte used subdued colours, without strong contrasts of light.

Francisco José de Goya y Lucientes (1746 - 1828), *Don Ramón Satué (1765 - 1824)*, 1823, canvas, 107 x 83.5 cm

Although the Rijksmuseum only possesses a single work by the Spanish artist Goya, it is an exceptional one. The painting is of Don Ramón Satué, a leading judge from Madrid. He is looking very relaxed, with his hands in his pockets. Goya needed very little colour for this painting, most of which is black. The red waistcoat is in striking contrast to the rest. Goya produced a rapid, lifelike portrait of this prominent Spanish magistrate.

Isaak Ouwater (1750 - 1793), *The Nieuwe Kerk and the rear façade of the town hall in Amsterdam*, before 1783, canvas, 59 x 73 cm

Ouwater's painting shows the Nieuwe Kerk (New Church) and the town hall (now the Palace on the Dam) as seen from the Nieuwezijds Voorburg-wal. On the western side of the church is the base of the Nieuwe Kerk steeple. This was never completed, and since it was in the way it was largely demolished in 1783; although undated, therefore, this picture must have been painted before then. Ouwater produced a very accurate, brick-by-brick rendering of this section of Amsterdam.

Jan van Huysum (1682 - 1740), *Still life with flowers and fruit*, c 1730, canvas, 80.5 x 62 cm

This wild bouquet, loosely arranged in a vase with some freshly picked fruit in front, was rendered with great precision by the flower artist Jan van Huysum. The odd insect and dewdrop make the flowers and fruit seem deceptively real. Yet this particular bouquet cannot have existed, since the flowers in it all bloom in different seasons: tulips, daffodils and anemones in spring, roses and carnations in summer, and scabious and tuberoses in autumn.

Adriaan de Lelie (1755 - 1820), *The art gallery of Jan Gil-demeester*, 1794 - 1795, panel, 63.5 x 85.7 cm

The walls of Jan Gildemeester's art gallery are hung from floor to ceiling with paintings. Gilde-meester was a fervent art collector. Here we see him amid his collection, which he is showing to friends and acquaintances in his house on the Herengracht in Amsterdam. Adriaan de Lelie depicted the scene so accurately that many of the paintings (which were sold off when Gildemeester died) are still identifiable. On the far right is a work by Rubens, which a visitor has climbed a step ladder to inspect more closely.

George van der Mijn (1726/1727 - 1763), *Antoinette Metayer*, 1759, canvas, 63 x 49 cm

This portrait of Antoinette Metayer by George van der Mijn is very unusual because the subject is gazing downwards. Antoinette is looking at the dog on her lap. But the dog is looking at us – sitting for its portrait, so to speak. This painting goes with the portrait of Antoinette's brother, Louis Metayer, which is also owned by the Rijks-museum. Metayer was an Amsterdam art collector and silversmith. In this picture Antoinette is 27 years old.

Cornelis Troost is the best-known eighteenth-century Dutch painter. At first he mostly painted portraits of wealthy citizens, but later he concentrated on scenes from stage plays. His source of inspiration for these was the Amsterdam Theatre, where he himself acted until 1724 and for which he also designed scenery. Only after he abandoned his stage career – he appears to have been a good actor – did the stage become the subject of his paintings. He mainly portrayed comedies from his own period as an actor. None of his 'theatre pieces' reveals that the scene is taking place on stage; instead, Troost located his actors in domestic interiors, streets or taverns.

Cornelis Troost (1696 - 1750), *The town garden, c 1745,* canvas, 66 x 56 cm

Theatrical staging is a striking feature of Troost's paintings. He portrayed his Amsterdam contemporaries against the backdrop of their own city, each playing his own role. *The town garden* is no exception. The artist has transformed this delightful spot into a 'stage': the house on the left looks like a piece of scenery, and the trees, sky and town house appear to have been painted on a backcloth. The leading roles in this charming scene are played by the father and his daughter.

Cornelis Troost (1696 - 1750), *The spendthrift*, 1741,
panel, 68.5 x 86 cm

This seemingly everyday scene in fact comes from
the play *The spendthrift*, by Thomas Asselijn. The
lady in the white dress, Joanna, is the spendthrift
in question. She sells her expensive clothes for
next to nothing, in return for jewellery. However,
her extravagance is discovered by her husband
and her father, who come to her door disguised as
Polish merchants. Troost offers us a colourful
portrayal of this farce, with plenty of details such
as the exotic animal on the left – a ring-tailed
lemur.

In Europe, the first half of the nineteenth century was the period of Romanticism. This trend emerged as a reaction to Classicism, which was felt to be impersonal and severe. Truth and feeling were the central themes of Romantic art. Wijnandus Nuyen was one of the few Dutch artists to paint in the truly Romantic style, with vigorous colours, dramatic subjects and strong contrasts. Other Dutch artists of the period were inspired by their illustrious predecessors from the seventeenth century, the Golden Age. This yearning for the past was another typical feature of Romanticism. Old masters were imitated and seventeenth-century subjects reinterpreted. Landscape painters such as Koekkoek and Schelfhout took their cue from the seventeenth-century Jacob van Ruisdael, while Cornelis Springer - the most famous of the nineteenth-century townscape painters - drew his inspiration from Berkheyde and Van der Heyden. In this way, nineteenth-century artists hoped to make their century a 'second Golden Age' of painting.

Wouter Johannes van Troostwijk (1782 - 1810), *The Raampoortje in Amsterdam*, 1809, canvas, 57 x 48 cm

Winter in Amsterdam. The steeple of the Westerkerk, shrouded in fog, is no more than a faint shadow behind the houses on the Bloemgracht. This painting by Van Troostwijk is an exceptional one, particularly for an early nineteenth-century artist. Instead of taking a prominent building or famous Amsterdam scene as his subject, he attempted to convey the atmosphere of a cold winter's day. This was very unusual for the time; half a century was to pass before artists in The Hague and Amsterdam again tried to capture mood and atmosphere in their paintings.

Josephus Augustus Knip (1777 - 1847), *The Bay of Naples, with the island of Ischia in the background*, 1818, canvas, 90 x 109 cm

This realistic-looking landscape shows Roman ruins with the island of Ischia in the background, off the coast of Naples. Knip stayed in Rome for two years and studied classical remains. On returning to the Netherlands, he used his drawings to produce this painting. To the left, half-overgrown, we can see the Colosseum. The arches are the remnants of Emperor Nero's aqueduct. Knip provided an accurate, smooth portrayal of this scene.

Pieter Gerardus van Os (1776 - 1839), *A watercourse near 's-Graveland*, 1818, canvas, 111.5 x 89.5 cm

As it intersects the polder, the canal forms a diagonal line within the composition of the painting. In the foreground we can see a man in an orchard, and two dogs playing. Van Os depicted the scene from above – probably from an attic window in the country home of the Amsterdam merchant Waller, who had asked him to come and paint the view. Van Os' main subjects were landscapes and cattle. What makes this painting such an exceptional instance of his work is its composition. This original work was very much ahead of its time. Its companion piece (also owned by the Rijksmuseum) shows a view across the meadows near 's-Graveland.

Wijnandus Johannes Josephus Nuyen (1813 - 1839),
River landscape with ruins, 1836, canvas, 99 x 141.5 cm

When he was twenty, Nuyen travelled to France.
There he met artists who painted in the Romantic
manner, with strong contrasts of light and shade,
intense colours and a sense of drama. Nuyen
became fascinated with this style of painting and
soon emerged as Holland's leading Romantic
artist. This painting is a good example of his
work, with a ruined castle, a dead tree blown
down by the wind, clouds scudding across the sky,
and shadows darkening the landscape. Nuyen's
work was innovative and exuberant by Dutch
standards.

Barend Cornelis Koekkoek (1803 - 1862), *Winter landscape*, 1838, canvas, 62 x 75 cm

In this painting there is snow everywhere: on the
roofs of the houses, on every tree, on every twig.
It is cold, but the sun is trying hard to break
through. Long shadows extend across the snowy
landscape. The famous landscape artist Koekkoek
attempted to imitate nature as closely as possible,
for he believed that nature embodied the truth.
However, his expertly composed paintings are not
realistic depictions of nature. He took the natural
scenery which he saw around him and deliberately idealized it.

Cornelis Springer (1817 - 1891) and **Kaspar Karsen** (1810 - 1896), *View of The Hague from the Delft Waterway in the seventeenth century*, 1852, canvas, 200 x 340 cm

Two painters worked together to produce this enormous view of The Hague, commissioned to decorate the Parkzaal in Amsterdam, where the inauguration of the statue of Rembrandt was to be celebrated. The painting shows The Hague as it must have looked in Rembrandt's day. However, despite Springer and Karsen's research into the subject, the scene is not entirely authentic: in the seventeenth century, just as in the nineteenth, the two mills that stood here were stone drainage mills, not wooden smock-mills as shown in the picture.

Cornelis Springer (1817 - 1891), *The Zuiderhavendijk in Enkhuizen*, 1868, panel, 50 x 65 cm

Cornelis Springer's depiction of the houses along the Zuiderhavendijk in Enkhuizen is extremely accurate. The different-coloured bricks used in the façades, the stone edgings contrasting with the brickwork, the facing bricks and even the patches of shadow on the houses were all rendered by Springer in minute detail. This Amsterdam artist was much in demand as a painter of townscapes, and was very prolific despite his disability (in 1857 he lost the sight in his right eye).

The years around 1850 saw the emergence of a new phenomenon in landscape painting. Dutch artists became acquainted with the work of the Barbizon School. These French painters, who were forerunners of the Impressionists, painted directly from nature ('en plein air'). Like their French counterparts, the Dutch artists chose wooded areas to paint in, and thus frequently congregated in such places as Oosterbeek, near Arnhem. Artists such as Bilders and Roelofs attempted to record nature as accurately as possible and to capture the mood of the moment in colour and light. After 1870, The Hague became the centre of a group of artists whose common element was nature, and who were to become known as the Hague School. These artists were not concerned with accurate renderings of the landscape, but with mood, light and colour.

Paul Joseph Constantin Gabriël (1828 - 1903), *A windmill on a polder waterway*, also known as *In the month of July*, 1889, canvas, 102 x 66 cm

A windmill is reflected in the water on a sweltering July day. Paul Gabriël's painting is a classical composition, emanating balance and tranquillity. He studied nature and was a careful observer of Dutch polder landscapes. But he also drew his inspiration from his seventeenth-century predecessors. Gabriël's windmill is quite as imposing as Ruisdael's mill at Wijk bij Duurstede. Both are viewed from below, standing out magnificently against a cloudy sky.

Albert Gerard Bilders (1838 - 1865), *Cows in the meadow*, canvas, 47 x 70 cm

Typical of Bilders' landscapes is their tranquil, intimate atmosphere. In this he resembles the French artists of the Barbizon School. After seeing an exhibition of their work in Brussels in 1860, he spent the final years of his brief life painting in the same style, attempting to record nature as accurately as possible and to capture the mood of the moment in colour and light. Bilders worked in Oosterbeek, in the company of other young artists. Oosterbeek was sometimes referred to as 'the Dutch Barbizon'.

Willem Maris (1844 - 1910), *Ducks*, c 1880, canvas, 93 x 113 cm

Ducks in the grass, and some more in the water behind them. Maris' rendering of the ducks' down and feathers is almost palpable. Ducks and cows were favourite subjects of this artist, who was the youngest of the Maris brothers. He was not so much concerned with lifelike portrayals of the actual animals as he was with light and atmosphere. Willem Maris is a typical painter of the Hague School.

Hendrik Johannes (later **Jan Hendrik) Weissenbruch** (1824 - 1903), *View of the shipping canal of Rijswijk, with the Binckhorst left and the Laakmolen right*, also known as *View near the Geestbrug*, 1868, panel, 31 x 50 cm

The point of this painting is not the actual landscape, but the atmosphere on a breezy summer's day. Overhead we can see a beautiful Dutch sky in numerous shades of blue, with light clouds blowing across it. The sunlight playing through the clouds is casting shadows on the countryside below. Weissenbruch was a member of the Hague School. These painters ventured out to paint nature as they found it close to where they lived, in and around The Hague.

Anton Mauve (1838 - 1888), *Morning ride on the beach,*
1876, canvas, 45 x 70 cm

A small group of horsemen is riding down to the
beach at Scheveningen. It must be about twelve
o'clock on a summer's day, for the shadows are
short. In this painting Mauve succeeds in con-
veying a magnificent sense of depth. The cart
tracks in the white sand lead the eye past another
horseman and out to the water's edge, where
some more tiny figures can just be seen. At the
foot of the dunes are some bathing machines –
Scheveningen was already increasingly popular as
a bathing resort. In this picture Anton Mauve
depicted a scene from fashionable cosmopolitan
life, which was unusual for him: he usually painted rural scenes.

Life in the capital was the Amsterdam impressionists' favourite subject. They painted people in the city - working, sitting in cafés or walking in the street. They were not concerned with lifelike portrayals - instead, they were attempting to capture a fleeting instant of a city in motion. They depicted their subjects in bright colours, with rapid brushwork and relatively little attention to detail. They painted city scenes in all kinds of weather, showing canals and squares in snow, rain or sunshine. To create an impression of speed and movement, the Amsterdam impressionists often painted people in close-up, as if they were walking out of the painting. They sometimes used photographs to help them.

George Hendrik Breitner (1857 - 1923), *Horse artillery*, canvas, 115 x 77.5 cm

This painting was purchased by the Rijksmuseum in 1886, just after the museum had moved to its present premises. Breitner must have painted it shortly before 1886. Military subjects appear in his work from 1880 onwards. Breitner was then living in The Hague, where he must often have seen military exercises along the beaches, but he also went to the southern province of Brabant to see larger, more spectacular exercises. This painting shows the artillerymen in action, galloping down from the dunes.

Isaac Lazarus Israëls (1865 - 1934), *Donkey-riding on the beach,* canvas, 51 x 70 cm

Isaac Israëls' picture of little girls riding donkeys on the beach was painted with loose brushwork, in cheerful colours. His light, rapid technique points to French influence. He made various journeys to France together with his father Jozef Israëls, and they were often visited by foreign artists. Israëls spent much of his life in Amsterdam, where he painted people in the street, in cafés and in theatres. In countless sketches he repeatedly attempted to capture the fleeting moment, to record precisely what he saw.

George Hendrik Breitner (1857 - 1923), *The bridge over the Singel at Paleisstraat, Amsterdam*, canvas, 100 x 152 cm

Here Breitner captured an instant of city life. People are walking along snowy streets, snugly wrapped in their winter coats. Breitner wanted to give the onlooker the impression of being there among the people in the street. He did this by abruptly curtailing the female figure in foreground, making it seem as though she was walking out of the picture. The city was in motion, and Breitner captured this motion in rapid brushstrokes, without much detail.

James Abbott McNeill Whistler (1834 - 1903), *Effie Deans*, also known as *Arrangement in yellow and grey*, c 1876, canvas, 194 x 93 cm

'She sunk her head upon her hand, and remained seemingly, unconscious as a statue - *The Heart of Mid Lothian* - Walter Scott.' This is what Whistler inscribed in the bottom left-hand corner of this painting of Effie Deans, the heroine from Walter Scott's 1818 novel. Whistler's mistress Maud Franklin was the model for Effie Deans. The long, high canvas, subdued colours and rapid brush-work are typical of Whistler's later work. Whistler, who was born in America, spent much of his life in Britain. He was one of the few great impressionists from outside France.

The Sculpture and Decorative Arts department has a particularly varied collection of sculptures in various materials, furniture, panelling, gold and silver, jewellery, earthenware, porcelain, glass, textiles, costumes, copper, bronze and iron objects, and much else besides. Although the main emphasis is on Dutch art, many parts of the collection have a sizeable international component. The collection differs in this respect from those of the Paintings and Dutch History departments.

The basis of the collection was the Royal Gallery of Rare Objects (founded in 1816), which had taken over large parts of collections formerly belonging to the stadholders. During the nineteenth century, this collection was extended by means of acquisitions and donations. In 1858, private benefactors set up the Royal Antiquarian Society in Amsterdam in order to establish a collection of antique decorative art. The Society operates on principles similar to those adopted by leading museums of decorative art in other countries, and permanent loans from its collection form a vital part of the department's exhibits.

When the Dutch Museum of History and Art was established in The Hague in 1875, a large number of items from the Royal Gallery of Rare Objects were added to its collection. In 1885, when the new Rijksmuseum building was opened, the Museum of History and Art was transferred to Amsterdam. At first, however, it remained a separate establishment within the Rijksmuseum, and was only absorbed into the Dutch History and Sculpture and Decorative Arts departments in 1927.

Following a period around 1900 in which a considerable amount of sculpture and decorative art was collected, there was little expansion in the 1920s and 1930s. However, things changed immediately after the Second World War, and an active acquisition policy has been pursued ever since, greatly enriching and expanding the department's collection. At the same time, the museum has been the grateful recipient of numerous private donations and bequests ranging from individual objects to extensive collections, both general and specialized. In 1952 the impressive collection established during the inter-war period by the German banker Fritz Mannheimer (1890 - 1939), who lived in Amsterdam, came into the Rijksmuseum's possession. This collection includes some magnificent drawings and paintings, but its most valuable feature is its unparalleled array of decorative art which, for all its diversity, is of almost unvaryingly high quality. The existing international character of the department was greatly enhanced by this acquisition, which made the Rijksmuseum's decorative art collection one of the greatest in the world. In recent decades, the department's acquisition policy has focused on objects from the nineteenth and early twentieth century, a period which is still underrepresented.

Sculpture

Key elements of the Sculpture collection are the medieval sculptures and wood carvings from the Netherlands and Dutch seventeenth-century sculpture, including the important set of terracotta sketches by Artus Quellinus for the decoration of Amsterdam's town hall (on permanent loan to the museum from the Amsterdam city authorities). There are also some important Italian bronzes and a considerable number of ivories.

Furniture

The Furniture collection is a magnificent selection of Dutch furniture up to the early nineteenth century. Particularly popular are the three dolls' houses: two extremely important seventeenth-century pieces and one from the eighteenth century. There is also an ample selection of French, German, Southern Netherlandish, Italian and English masterpieces, mainly dating from the seventeenth and eighteenth century and most of them originally part of the Mannheimer collection.

Gold and silver

The museum's Gold and silver collection again focuses on the Netherlands, with the main emphasis on the great masters of the early seventeenth century: the Van Vianen brothers and Johannes Lutma. Other significant items are German gold and silver from the sixteenth and seventeenth century and early nine-teenth-century French silver.

The Jewellery collection concentrates on two periods, the Renaissance and Art Nouveau, in both cases including internationally renowned works of art.

Jewellery

The main items in the Ceramics collection are delftware (an extremely important collection of which was donated in 1916 by the heirs of J.F. Loudon), Meissen porcelain (most of it from the Mannheimer collection) and Dutch porcelain. There is also some fine Italian majolica, German stoneware and porcelain from numerous other European factories.

Ceramics

The Glass collection focuses on Dutch engraved glass, including a particularly rich selection of work by famous engravers from the seventeenth and eighteenth century. Many pieces are from the bequest by A.J. Enschedé in 1896 as well as other donations and bequests. Besides Dutch glass, there are also some fine examples of Italian and German work.

Glass

The Textile collection includes a considerable number of tapestries. In addition to rare products by the main Dutch workshops, there are some excellent examples from leading European textile centres. The outstanding collection of linen damask is a particularly famous item.

Textile

The Costume collection is largely made up of donations and bequests. A major addition was the large donation by Mrs. C.I. Six in 1978. This collection is mainly Dutch, focusing on clothing and accessories either produced or worn in this country.

Costume

The Copper and bronze collection includes an important group of aquamaniles from the thirteenth and fourteenth century.

Copper and bronze

Such a brief review can scarcely do justice to the wealth of the various collections, and many of the objects illustrated in this book fall outside the main categories mentioned here. Examples are the French gold triptych (p. 85), the alabaster annunciation by Tilman Riemenschneider (p. 87), the Buglioni retable (p. 92), the Italian jasper drinking-vessel (p. 95), the enamelled pocket-watch by Toutin (p. 96), and Falconet's sculpture *L'Amour menaçant* (p. 115).

Most surviving items of medieval decorative art belonged to either the nobility or the Church, the only patrons of any significance until urban life began to revive in the thirteenth century. The growth of the cities caused arts and sciences to blossom; craftsmen formed guilds and received commissions from city councils, the Church, other guilds and wealthy citizens.

A central feature of all medieval life was religion, and art was no exception. There was a predilection for depictions of Christ and the Virgin Mary, who acquired increasingly human traits in the late Middle Ages. The suffering of Christ particularly appealed to people's imagination. Saints and their relics were also considered important, and costly reliquaries were made for them as a sign of veneration.

∧
Tympanum from the church of Egmond abbey, Holland, c 1120 - 1140, variegated sandstone, lead (pupils of St. Peter's eyes), 88 x 175 x 12.5 cm

Aquamanile in the form of a knight on horseback, Hildesheim, Lower Saxony, first half of the thirteenth century, bronze or brass, 32 x 27 x 14.8 cm

This relief comes from the abbey church of St. Peter and St. Adelbert in Egmond, where the counts of Holland were buried. Here we see St. Peter with Count Dirk VI of Holland to the left and the Count's mother, Countess Petronella, to the right. St. Peter, who can be identified by his key and his round face with its fringe of curly beard, was the gatekeeper of heaven. The inscription informs us that Petronella and Dirk are imploring him to admit them. This relief, which was originally a memorial slab, was probably made by a monk.

An aquamanile is a water vessel – usually in the form of an animal – which was used to wash one's hands at meals or during Mass. In this case, there was originally a spout with a tap coming out of the knight's chest. The spout is now missing, as are the knight's helmet, shield and sword. The aquamanile was cast using the *cire perdue* (lost-wax) technique, in which the wax model melted away when heated. This meant that only one cast could be made.

Reliquary in the form of a bust of St. Frederick, **Elyas Scerpswert,** Utrecht, 1326, silver, partly gilded, 45 x 24 cm

This bust is sometimes referred to as a 'speaking' reliquary, because the shape indicates what it contained – in this case, a piece of the skull of Bishop Frederick of Utrecht, who is said to have been murdered in 838 together with his assistant Odulphus. When their graves in the St. Salvator (Holy Saviour) Church in Utrecht were restored in 1362, this reliquary was commissioned from the silversmith Elyas Scerpswert. Using a variety of techniques, he created a magnificent work of art, which he signed on the base.

Triptych, Paris (?), c 1400, gold and enamel, 12.7 x 12.5 cm (opened out)

This altarpiece was intended for private devotion. The figure of Christ as the Man of Sorrows stimulated the imagination. In the middle we see Christ displaying his wounds. On the wings are the Virgin Mary and St. John, with angels carrying the instruments of Christ's suffering: the Cross, the spear and the nails. This miniature triptych – an example of court painting – is a magnificent piece of craftsmanship. Various enamelling techniques were applied, including the complicated *émail en ronde-bosse,* or encrusted enamelling; this was used for the figure of Christ, which is completely covered with enamel.

Christ descending into limbo, Southern Netherlands or Northern France, c 1440, oak, with polychrome and gilding, 48.5 cm (group); 97.8 x 58.9 x 22.3 (frame)

Christ is standing on the door of limbo, which has fallen to the ground. Limbo is the place where the dead who have not yet been admitted to heaven must stay. The devil is lying crushed beneath the door. Christ is reaching out to Adam, who is the first to emerge from the fiery mouth of hell. Others are waiting their turn. The group was placed in a Gothic frame, which was part of a large altarpiece.

The meeting of the Magi, **Adriaen van Wesel** (c 1417 - c 1490), Utrecht, c 1475 - 1477, oak, traces of polychrome, 76.5 x 91 x approx. 20 cm

The Magi are meeting before setting out together on their journey to Bethlehem to worship the newborn infant Jesus. They have arrived from three different directions, and their horses are almost touching each other. This rendering of their meeting is extremely vivid. The king arriving from the left is being stared at by shepherds with their flocks; arriving from the top is the Moorish king; and the king on the right is just dismounting. Such expressiveness is typical of Van Wesel, who was the leading North Netherlandish sculptor in the late Middle Ages.

<

Catharina, **Master of Koudewater** (active c 1460 - 1480), 's-Hertogenbosch, c 1470, walnut with polychrome, 92 cm

Catharina is standing on a small man who has a crown on his head and a sceptre in his hand. This man is emperor Maxentius who made her debate with fifty pagan philosophers in order to convince her to renounce the true faith. To no avail: the fifty converted to Christianity themselves. The unicorn on her necklace symbolises Catharina's devotion to Christ. Catharina is one of a group of four statues of saints in the Rijksmuseum made by the same sculptor. They originate from a monastery in Koudewater.

>

Statuette of unknown woman, one of ten mourners from the tomb of Isabella of Bourbon, South Brabant, 1476, bronze, 58 cm

A lady of distinction, with a very striking head-dress. She is holding both hands and one arm tightly against her body to keep her clothes together. These are excessively long for the fashion of the day. Equally fashionable is her head-dress: a V-shaped *bourrelet* ('cloth sausage') with a piece of cloth to hold it in place. The statuette – one of the mourning figures that decorated the tomb of Isabella of Bourbon in Antwerp – probably represents Anne, Countess of Belfort.

The annunciation, **Tilman Riemenschneider** (c 1460 - 1531), Southern Germany, c 1480 - 1485, alabaster, with partial polychrome and gilding, 39 cm and 40.5 cm

We can see that the angel has only just landed – he is crouching on one knee and the edge of his cope is flying up. In his left hand is a banderole bearing the words AVE MAR(IA) (Hail Mary). The Virgin is looking up in astonishment from the lectern at which she is kneeling in her cloak. Riemenschneider rendered this event vividly, with great attention to facial expression and other details. This is characteristic of his style. This group is one of his most important early works.

Hood from a cope with the dispute of St. Catherine, Netherlands, c 1525, linen, silk, gold thread and pearls, 53 x 49 cm

St. Catherine was a princess who converted to Christianity around 300. Hagiography relates that the Roman emperor Maxentius tried to make her renounce her faith by having her debate with 50 philosophers. However, St. Catherine succeeded in convincing and even converting her adversaries, who were all promptly burnt at the stake. St. Catherine was beheaded. This work is a magnificent example of the sophisticated couching-stitch technique, in which gold thread was fastened to the material with silk threads in various colours. The effect of light and shade was achieved by varying the distance between the stitches.

Oak dresser, Netherlands, c 1525, oak, 147 x 103.5 x 74.5 cm

This dresser, which is open at the bottom, is Gothic in style. This can be seen from its shape, recalling the chest from which this piece of furniture evolved. The decorations are also Gothic, with fluted motifs on the side and rear panels and tracery (borrowed from Gothic church windows) at the front. The tracery contains various symbols referring to Charles V: the lily, the imperial crown, the royal crown and what is known as the flint-and-steel with crossed arrows. The dresser comes from the Guild of the Civic Guard in Alkmaar.

>
Tapestry showing the washing of St. Peter's feet, workshop of **Pieter van Aelst**, Brussels, 1511 - 1518, from a cartoon dated 1507, wool, silk and gold thread, 299 x 311 cm

Christ is about to wash the feet of the apostle Peter, who is appalled and is raising his hands in a gesture of refusal. The washing of the feet is the main event depicted in this tapestry, which includes three other episodes from the Passion of Christ. The tapestry is part of a larger series. The illusion of reality was achieved by the use of refined materials and the alternation of light and dark tones.

Tapestry showing Procris taking leave of Diana, **François Spiering,** after a design by **Karel van Mander,** Delft, c 1610, linen, wool and silk, 345 x 520 cm

This tapestry illustrates episodes from the tale of Cephalus and Procris. Cephalus, disguised as someone else, seduces his wife and then accuses her of infidelity. In consternation, Procris takes refuge with the goddess Diana and her nymphs, but eventually decides to return to her husband. The tapestry is part of a 'Diana series' woven by François Spiering, an Antwerp weaver who settled in Delft, thereby giving an enormous boost to the Dutch tapestry-weaving industry.

Goblet with lid, with the arms of Von Schwindt, **Anno Knütgen,** Siegburg, 1577, stoneware, 31 cm

Mortar, attributed to **Willem Wegewart the Elder,** Deventer, 1568, bronze, 22.4 cm, diam. 21.6 cm

This goblet is made of stoneware, a particularly hard, waterproof type of pottery produced in the Rhineland. Typical features of sixteenth-century products from Siegburg are the buff-coloured glaze and moulded decorations, in this case alternating with stamped ornamentation. The principal motifs on this goblet are lions and coats of arms. On the belly of the goblet we can see the arms of Von Schwindt and the year of manufacture.

This mortar bears the inscription: GERRIT TONISSEN HEFT MI LATEN GIETEN AO 1568 (Gerrrit Tonissen had me cast anno 1568). Tonissen probably had this done by Willem Wegewart the Elder, a caster of bells and artillery-pieces from Deventer. Characteristic of this artist's work are the friezes decorated with foliage and the fanciful escutcheons, one of which contains the monogram EV. Like the vase in the bottom frieze, these are typical Renaissance motifs.

Retable with Madonna and Child between St. Jerome and St. Nicholas of Myra, **Benedetto Buglioni** (1459/1460 - 1521), Florence, 1502, majolica, 226 x 172 cm

This altarpiece is made of majolica (tin-glazed, multi-coloured pottery), in a style made famous by the Florentine Della Robbia family. It is made up of several different reliefs. The classical-looking frame is typical of the Renaissance, as is the lifelike appearance of the figures (the Madonna and Child, St. Jerome and St. Nicholas). The socle shows scenes from their lives; on the right, St. Nicholas is throwing the three poor maidens golden orbs for their dowries.

Dish showing 'Calumny' by Apelles, **Nicolà da Urbino** (died after 1537/1538), Urbino, c 1520/1525, majolica, diam. 53 cm

This illustration is based on a description of the most famous painting from antiquity, 'Calumny', by the Greek artist Apelles. Calumny has dragged an innocent young man before the judge, who has ass's ears and is assisted by figures representing Ignorance and Suspicion. Calumny herself is surrounded by Deceit, Malice and Envy. Standing aside from all this is the naked Truth. Nicolà da Urbino's illustration of this tale is extremely vivid. His nickname, 'the Raphael of majolica', was well-earned.

Albarello bearing the inscription TIRICA.MA.G, Antwerp, c 1525/1550, majolica, 26 cm

In the sixteenth century Italian potters settled in cities in the Southern Netherlands, where they proceeded to produce majolica objects exactly like those back in their homeland. This albarello, or apothecary's jar, was made in Antwerp. Painted on it are a hare, a stag, decorative borders and a diagonal band. The latter, as well as the upper border, are typical of Antwerp. The inscription refers to the contents of the jar: Theriaca Magna, a universal antidote.

Bust of Pope Gregory XIV, **Sebastiano Torrigiani** (worked in Rome from 1573 - 1596), Rome, 1590 - 1591, bronze, 31 cm

The Pope is shown here in full regalia, with his cope and alb (a white linen vestment) and the papal tiara on his head. The border of the cope is decorated with illustrations of saints. This bust follows the characteristic form of Mannerist sculpture, with a tapering chest ending in a cherub's head. Beneath this is the inscription GRE-XIV. Torrigiani was one of a group of bronze-casters who received important commissions from the Pope.

Silversmiths flourished in the sixteenth century, thanks to commissions from churches, nobility, urban patricians, governments and guilds. Many of the magnificent pieces produced for such patrons borrowed their form and decorative features from architecture: first the classical formal language of the Renaissance, and later the artificial and exaggerated version of this known as Mannerism. A characteristic feature of this period was an interest in science and nature, expressed among other things in the use of costly types of stone or exotic materials such as shells or buffalo horn. Leading centres for goldsmiths and silversmiths were the South German cities of Augsburg, Munich and Nuremberg.

Drinking-horn of the Amsterdam Guild of Arquebusiers, attributed to **Arent Coster** (recorded between 1521 and 1563), Amsterdam, 1547, buffalo horn and silver, 37.5 cm

This drinking-horn, which was the showpiece of the Amsterdam Guild of Arquebusiers (a civic guard association), was used on ceremonial occasions. Their emblem – a bird's claw – is incorporated in the silver band around the horn. At the top are the Dutch Lion and the coat of arms of Amsterdam. The horn is resting on a tree-trunk flanked by a lion and a dragon, which appear in the family coat of arms of the donor, Van der Schelling.

Table ornament, **Wenzel Jamnitzer** (1508 - 1585), Nuremberg, 1549, silver, partly gilded, and enamel, 99.8 cm

Mother Earth is standing on a rock which is overgrown with all kinds of plants and grasses. Above her head she is holding a large metal dish, which is likewise decorated with her progeny, all rendered in minute detail. The object is made entirely of silver, and was originally painted in lifelike colours. All the miniature flora and fauna are casts taken from actual plants and animals. Jamnitzer was world-famous for his flawless technique. This ornament, originally meant as a gift for Emperor Charles V, is one of Jamnitzer's largest and most important works.

Decorative vessel in the form of a monster, probably from the Sarachi workshop, Milan, first quarter of the seventeenth century, jasper, gold, enamel and precious stones, 18 x 28 cm

This vessel consists of five pieces of jasper which form the feet, body, tail, wings and head of a dragon-like monster. The beast's gaping jaws allow the vessel to be used as a lamp. The wings are the lid. The costly materials and whimsical form are typically Mannerist. Such ingenious objects were intended purely for decoration and were exhibited in *galleries* belonging to private collectors.

Pendant with wedding symbols, South Germany, c 1600, gold, enamel, diamonds and pearls, 10 x 6 cm

The precious stones in this pendant are all diamonds, including a large stone in a rectangular setting at the centre. Diamonds are traditional symbols of marital fidelity. The other decorations also make it clear that this is a wedding pendant: two right hands encircling a blazing heart, two turtledoves and two parakeets. The cornucopias are references to love and fertility. The only things which are inexplicable are the eagle and the thunderbolts - symbols of the god Jupiter.

Double goblet, **Hans Petzolt** (1551 - 1633), Nuremberg, late sixteenth century, silver-gilt, 54 cm

This 'double goblet' consists of two separate goblets. They are identical, except that the upper goblet has a slightly wider rim which allows it to fit neatly over the lower one. The rims of the goblets are marked with an inscription and the year 1596. Petzolt's decoration of hemispheres and scrolled foliage harks back to the Gothic period, but he also used Renaissance motifs.

Tableau of tiles showing warriors in a circle, Holland,
c 1580 - 1620, majolica, 108.5 x 81.5 cm

The art of making majolica – pottery with a white
tin glaze – had been brought to Antwerp from
Italy in the sixteenth century. Majolica and tile
makers also became established in Holland from
1580 onwards. A typically Dutch product is the
majolica wall tile, a functional item in damp
houses. These particular tiles are each decorated
with a soldier bearing a lance, musket or drum.
The decoration in the corner is a quarter of a
larger decoration formed by four tiles.

*Pocket-watch with allegories on the marriage of Prince Wil-
liam II of Orange and Princess Mary Stuart in 1641*, **Henry
Toutin** (painting) and **Antoine Masurier** (movement), Paris,
c 1641, gold and enamel, diam. 6.4 cm

This watch probably belonged to the
bridegroom's father, Prince Frederick Henry.
Painted all over it in enamel are scenes relating to
his son's marriage to the English princess. On the
inside of the cover is the wedding ceremony,
while the dial shows two cupids bringing flowers
for the happy couple. The technique of enamel
painting on gold, which was new at the time, was
Henry Toutin's speciality.

Dish showing a ship being attacked by a monster, Holland, c 1620 - 1645, majolica, diam. 33.8 cm

Painted on the white tin glaze of this earthenware dish is a typically Dutch scene: an East Indiaman at sea, flying the Dutch flag. In this case, however, the ship is being attacked by a monster. This illustrates the fact that Holland's glorious sea trade was not without its dangers. The rim of the dish is decorated with aigrettes (ornaments representing a precious stone with a plume of feathers). The back of the dish is covered with a transparent lead glaze.

Rummer with diamond engraving, **Anna Roemers** (1583 - 1651), Netherlands, 1621, dark green glass, 13 cm, diam. 6 cm

In the seventeenth century, glass-engraving was popular among upper-class women. Anna Roemers, who decorated this rummer with a diamond graver, was the daughter of the poet Roemer Visscher and, like her father, was artistically talented. Among her illustrations of a wild rose, a carnation, a marigold, a dragonfly and a shell, which she took from a book of samples, she engraved a dedication in Italian. Such beautifully decorated glassware was often intended as a gift.

Cabinet, decorated with paintings, attributed to **Frans Francken** II, Antwerp, cabinet first half of seventeenth century, stand second half of seventeenth century, limewood and oak, decorated with ebony, tortoiseshell, ivory, silver and mirrors, 159 x 109 x 49.5 cm

In the sixteenth and seventeenth century, collecting art and curios became so popular that special cabinets with numerous drawers and compartments were made to store the collections. The paintings that decorate this art cabinet show scenes from the Book of Genesis, with Adam and Eve and their sons Cain and Abel. The fact that the paintings can only be seen when the doors and lid are open increases the element of surprise.

Dolls' house belonging to Petronella Oortman, Netherlands, c 1690, oak, with tortoiseshell and tin veneer; interior made of various precious materials, 255 x 189.5 x 78 cm

This was not a dolls' house for children to play with, but an art gallery which was 'open to the public'. It was already famous by the early eighteenth century and has remained so, for it is the most lavishly executed and most realistic surviving dolls' house. It is laid out just like a real seventeenth-century house, with miniature items of furniture, a collection of china in the show kitchen, a library of tiny books (complete with texts) and a fully-equipped lying-in room. The best room is painted all over, with landscapes on the walls and birds in the sky on the ceiling. The outside of the cabinet is equally beautiful, being entirely covered with an ingeniously patterned tortoiseshell and tin veneer.

Rocking cradle, Sri Lanka, second half of seventeenth century, ebony and ivory, 90 x 135 cm

This cradle comes from Ceylon (now Sri Lanka), which at the time was partly under Dutch administration. It is made entirely of ebony, and decorated with ivory carvings and inlays. The cradle is a mixture of Western and Oriental design. The general shape and the turning of the bars are European, but the carved motifs are Ceylonese snakes, fish and elephants, which are symbols of water, fertility and youth. The Ceylonese were celebrated carvers of wood and ivory.

Tabletop, **Michiel Verbiest** and **Peter de Loose,** Antwerp, 1689, oak decorated with tortoiseshell, copper, brass, tin and mother-of-pearl, 88 x 148 cm

This tabletop is decorated with marquetry made of tortoiseshell, various metals and mother-of-pearl, also known as boulle (buhl) marquetry after the famous French furniture-maker André-Charles Boulle (1642 – 1732). This technique required great skill, as the various pieces had to fit together like a jigsaw puzzle. This particular tabletop was inlaid with motifs of vines, flower tendrils, putti (cupids), birds and monkeys within a basic pattern of scrolls. The coats of arms are those of Simon de Neuf and his wife Jacoba Martina van Eversdijk. The work is signed and dated on one of the tulip leaves.

Oak cabinet, attributed to **Jan van Mekeren** (1658 - 1733), Amsterdam, c 1690 - 1710, oak veneered with kingwood, ebony, rosewood, olivewood, maple and other types of wood, 205 x 173 x 61 cm

In comparison with cabinets that are decorated with statues or raised panelling, this cabinet, which has a high base, is very simple in its design. Every part is as flat as possible, thus focusing attention on the flower pattern of the marquetry. The cabinet is attributed to Jan van Mekeren, who enjoyed a fine reputation in this field. His flower patterns are almost like paintings, with the same compositions of flowers in a vase surrounded by butterflies and birds, just the way painters made them.

Table, The Hague (?), c 1700, limewood (base) and oak (top), gilded, 87.5 x 108.5 x 73.5 cm

The legs of this console table are in the form of S-shaped herms – half-figure, half-support – representing the four seasons. The opulent style of the table is characteristic of the Dutch version of the Louis XIV style, of which Daniel Marot was the leading exponent. This table shows strong French influence and was probably made in The Hague by French Huguenots.

^

Dish showing the story of Diana and Actaeon, by **Paulus van Vianen** (c 1570 - 1613), Prague, 1613, silver, 52 x 40.8 cm

This dish depicts the fate of the hunter Actaeon, who spied on the goddess Diana as she was bathing. She punished him by turning him into a stag, whereupon he was seized on and torn to pieces by his own hounds. This scene is shown on the back of the dish. The edge is decorated in the new, 'fleshy' lobate style. The dish and a matching jug were the last objects that Paulus made.

>

Memorial jug, by **Adam van Vianen** (1568/1569 - 1627), Utrecht, 1614, silver-gilt, 25.5 cm

Paulus van Vianen died in 1613, and the Amsterdam Goldsmiths' and Silversmiths' Guild commissioned this jug from Adam van Vianen in memory of his brother. The jug – made from a single sheet of silver, except for the lid – was produced entirely in the lobate style of decoration introduced by Paulus. The use of this style resulted in a novel shape, in which various different figures merge with one another.

The seventeenth century was the Golden Age of Dutch goldsmiths and silversmiths. Leading artists in this field were the Van Vianen brothers, Adam and Paulus. Adam stayed in Utrecht, but his younger brother went to Prague, where he worked at the court of the German Emperor Rudolph II. Paulus was not only a skilled craftsman, but a gifted artist who achieved such life-like effects with his 'chasing' technique that the objects he created almost seem like paintings in silver. Equally original was his use of what is known as in Dutch as kwabornament (the 'lobate' style of ornamentation) for the edges and other parts of dishes and jugs. Skin, bone and flabby rolls of flesh must have been the source of inspiration for this form of decoration, which became extremely popular in the Netherlands. Paulus' brother Adam made an entire jug in the lobate style, of which splendid examples can also be found in the work of the Amsterdam silversmith Johannes Lutma.

Jug and dish with maritime scenes, by **Johannes Lutma the Elder** (1587 - 1669), Amsterdam, 1647, silver, jug: 50.4 cm; dish: diam. 70 cm

This jug and dish are decorated with lobate ornamentation and marine motifs: children mounted on sea creatures, shells, mermaids and tritons. The set was probably made to commemorate one of the naval exploits of Admiral Maarten Harpertsz Tromp. The coat of arms in the centre of the dish belongs to his son Cornelis, who was also an admiral. Here the lobate style has developed into an elaborate Baroque design. This set is Lutma's most monumental work and a magnificent example of ornate Amsterdam metalware.

Two salt cellars, by **Adam van Vianen** (1568/1569 - 1627), Utrecht, 1620 and 1621, silver, 26 cm

From time immemorial salt was thought to be an almost holy substance and an essential food. The salt cellar as a costly table ornament also has a long tradition. Adam van Vianen gave this set of salt cellars a sculptural look in which the small dishes are integrated into the figural presentations on the stem to form a whole. One cellar shows Cain about to slay Abel, the other Abraham's sacrifice.

Two salt cellars, by **Johannes Lutma the Elder** (1587 - 1669), Amsterdam, 1639, silver, partly gilded, 23.4 cm

Lutma was quite obviously influenced by the Van Vianen brothers. These salt cellars have the same structure as Adam van Vianen's: the same foot, the same figure bearing a dish, and the same lobate decoration. However, Lutma made a clear distinction between the various parts. His theme here was the sea, with dishes in the shape of shells carried by children on dolphins. These salt cellars are among the best of Lutma's work. He evidently thought so too, for he had his portrait painted with one of them.

Shortly after 1600, the Dutch East India Company began importing porcelain from China. This had a major effect on the development of Dutch earthenware, or majolica. Driven by the competition of porcelain, most majolica makers reduced dishware production and expanded tile production as there was no competition in that area.

Two Delft companies took a different path: they improved the majolica so that it resembled Chinese porcelain and called their product 'Dutch porceleyn'. They did excellent business when civil war broke out in China in 1647, leaving the porcelain kilns dormant and causing exports to dry up. Many others followed their lead and around 1660 approximately 25 factories were mass producing blue faience with Chinese decoration. After 1680/1685 tastes changed and multi-coloured faience was also made available. In the period after 1725 the number of factories diminished gradually, due at first to heavy competition from the new English creamware (Wedgwood) and European porcelain discovered in Saxony.

Wine cooler with two bottles, **Lambert van Eenhoorn**, 'De Metalen Pot' factory, or **Louwijs Fictoor**, 'De Dobbelde Schenckan' factory, Delft, c 1695 - 1720, faience, 32 cm

The two bottles are identical in shape, with a high foot and a body which is flat on one side and rounded on the other. This enables them to fit perfectly into the oval wine cooler, which is also partitioned across the middle. The same blue, red and green decorations appear on the cooler and the bottles. Some of these - such as the cartouches and garlands - are European, but others were inspired by Chinese motifs.

Teapot with chinoiserie, **Rochus Jacobsz Hoppesteyn** (? - 1692), 'Het Moriaenshooft' factory, Delft, c 1685 - 1690, faience, 17,2 x 18,5 cm

This teapot is decorated on either side with an impression of a racing dear. In addition, it is decorated with scattered motifs borrowed from Chinese porcelain. The blue and green colours of the decoration blended with the (white) glaze during firing, but the gold and red colours were applied later and fired at a much lower temperature, a process invented by the Hoppesteyn family around 1680. This teapot was probably only used for ornamental purposes. Shaped like a Chinese wine jug, it barely resembles the imitation Chinese teapots produced at other factories in Delft.

Violin, attributed to **Dammas Hofdijck**, 'De Roos' factory, Delft, c 1690 - 1720, faience, 63 x 22 cm

Despite the increasing popularity of multi-coloured delftware, the blue variety continued to be produced, but with the emphasis on unusual objects. This violin, of which only four examples are known, is a miracle of technical skill and extremely attractive to look at. Painted into the glaze are scenes of music and dancing: a group of people dancing in an elegant interior, and peasants dancing in a tavern.

Wedding dress, France, c 1759, rep silk, embroidered with multi-coloured silk, 140.5 x 230 cm, waist 58 cm, train 216.5 x 153.5 cm

This light-blue dress is said to have been worn by Helena Slicher at her wedding to Aelbrecht Baron van Slingelandt in The Hague in 1759. It is a gala dress consisting of a bodice with a short train, a skirt and a loose train. The fashion at the time was a narrow waist and broad hips, which were further accentuated by means of panniers worn over the undergarment.

Wall clock showing Time vanquishing Love, **Charles Cressent** (1685 - 1768), Paris, c 1730, gilded bronze, 110 x 50.5 cm

Although Charles Cressent is mainly known as a maker of furniture, his skill as a sculptor is well demonstrated by this cartel-pendule, a wall clock in the shape of an escutcheon (cartel = escutcheon). At the top of this elegant, whimsical timepiece in the asymmetrical Rococo style is the menacing figure of Father Time, brandishing his scythe. His intended prey is Cupid, the naked toddler underneath the dial, who has dropped his bow and arrow in fright.

Snuffbox, **Lazare-Antoine Clérin** (1741 - 1782), Paris (?), 1751/1752, gold and enamel, 7.2 x 5.3 x 3.4 cm

The hatched background of this rectangular box is decorated with bouquets of flowers in enamel. The foliage around the edges is characteristic of the Louis XVI style. This snuffbox is thus an early example of the newly emerging style, at a time when the Rococo or Louis XV style still prevailed in other materials. Gold boxes such as this were decorated in accordance with the very latest fashion.

Tapestry showing Cupid with two torches in a medallion, designed by **François Boucher, Maurice Jacques** and **Louis Tessier** (border), Manufacture Royale des Gobelins, Paris, 1776 - 1784, wool and silk, 370 x 235 cm

François Boucher (1703 – 1770) was one of the great French Rococo painters and court painter to Louis XV. He painted in an exuberant style, with a predilection for pastel shades. Love was a favourite theme at this time, and this tapestry shows Cupid using a burning-glass to light a torch, a symbol of awakening love. The composition of the tapestry is virtually symmetrical, which is characteristic of the Louis XVI style.

Goblet with lid, engraved on the wheel by **Jacob Sang** (c 1720 - ?), Amsterdam, 1768, clear glass, 28.9 cm, diam. 10.3 cm

This glass shows the reclamation of the Watergraafs-meer (a lake between Diemen and Amsterdam), with the lake on one side and the newly reclaimed land on the other, including the road known as the Middelweg (now the Middenweg in east Amsterdam). The Latin inscription reads 'Reborn from the waves, let it prosper'. This is one of the best works by Jacob Sang, who specialized in wheel engraving (a method involving a small revolving wheel).

<

Goblet showing the arms of the States General and the flag of the United States of America, England (glass), Netherlands (engraving), 1782, clear glass, 18.5 cm, diam. 10 cm

This glass was engraved to mark the recognition of the United States of America by the States General of the Seven United Provinces (the Netherlands) on 19 April 1782. The two medallions, which are tied together with a ribbon, show the Dutch coat of arms (left) and the American flag flying from a citadel (right). The glass probably came from England, but was engraved in the Netherlands.

^

Wainscoting and furniture, designed by **Abraham van der Hart** (1747 - 1820), Amsterdam, c 1793 - 1795, 425 x 970 x 500 cm

This reception room at the home of the wealthy Haarlem businessman Willem Kops has survived intact, complete with wainscoting, wall coverings, carpet, curtains, 19 pieces of furniture, candelabras and a chandelier. The interior was designed by the Amsterdam city architect Van der Hart in the French Louis XVI style - rectilinear and elegant, with decorations inspired by classical models. The silk fabrics were ordered from France and the carpet seemingly from Tournai, but the wainscoting and furniture were probably made in Amsterdam, in imitation of French originals.

France and the French court remained the centre of attention in the eighteenth century. This was the century of the Louis XIV, XV and XVI styles, called after the three successive kings of that name. The heavy style of Louis XIV's court persisted in the Netherlands for quite some time, but a reaction set in around 1730. Furniture then became light and slender, with curved legs, arching lines and asymmetrical decoration. This style was called Louis XV, but was also known as Rococo (from the French rocaille = decorative rock or shell work). This was the name used in Germany, where the style was adopted by numerous furniture-makers. A reaction to the elegant frivolity of Rococo set in around 1770. The new style was the 'noble simplicity' of classical antiquity: austere lines, straight, tapering legs, and symmetrical decoration based on motifs borrowed from antiquity. This was known as the neoclassical or Louis XVI style.

In addition to France, a constant source of inspiration was the Orient; this was reflected, for example, in the use of lacquer panels.

Cutlery case, mounting by **Johannes Schiotling**, Amsterdam, 1772, mahogany and oak (base), silver, 36 x 29 x 21.6 cm

Expensive cutlery cases such as this were often made in the Netherlands in the second half of the eighteenth century. The silverware was displayed in the open case on a sideboard in the same style. This particular case, with its curved sides, is a fine example of the Rococo style. The mounting, with its asymmetrical design, C-shaped scrolls and motifs borrowed from nature, is very much in keeping with the rest. The silversmith, Johannes Schiotling, originally came from Sweden.

Simplicia cabinet, Netherlands, 1730, oak, inlaid with burr
walnut, 207.5 x 93 x 71.5 cm

When closed, this cabinet looks like a typical
Dutch eighteenth-century storage cabinet with
drawers in the middle section. Yet, when opened
up, the upper section turns out to be a miniature
pharmacy, with innumerable drawers and no
fewer than 148 vials, 61 wooden casks and 92
delftware apothecaries' jars. These were originally
all filled with *simplicia*, or simples (raw materials
from which medicines were made). The cabinet
belonged to the Delft Apothecaries' Guild and
was used during examinations.

Writing table, by **Abraham Roentgen** (1711 - 1795), Neuwied, c 1765, oak, maple and walnut, veneered with various types of wood, tortoiseshell, silver, mother-of-pearl, copper and bone, with gilded bronze mounting, 148.5 x 113 x 62 cm

This truly magnificent writing table displays all the flamboyant elegance of the Rococo style, is ingeniously constructed and is decorated all over with marquetry. Its opulence is enhanced by the gilded bronze mounting. This piece of furniture was made for Johann Philipp von Walderdorff, Elector and Archbishop of Trier. Particularly unusual features are the hinged components which extend at the touch of a concealed button. Abraham Roentgen and later his son David were famous throughout Europe.

Seated Cupid: l'Amour menaçant (Love threatens), **Etienne-Maurice Falconet** (1716 - 1791), Paris, 1757, marble, 87 cm, including base 185 cm

Writing table, attributed to **Adam Weisweiler** (1744 - 1820), Paris, c 1780 - 1790, oak, veneered with ebony, Japanese lacquer panels, red-veined marble and gilded bronze mounting, 132 x 88 cm

When Madame de Pompadour saw a similar statue made of terracotta, she commissioned a marble version from Falconet. It was to become one of the most popular French eighteenth-century sculptures: a mischievous Cupid holding his finger to his lips as though saying 'shhh', while pulling an arrow from his quiver with his other hand. The words by Voltaire inscribed on the pedestal makes him seem all the more threatening: 'Whoever you may be, behold your Master - past, present or future.'

Compared with the flamboyant Rococo style, this writing table is austere and rectilinear – typical features of the neoclassical Louis XVI style, which took its inspiration from classical antiquity. This can be seen in the legs, which resemble tapering columns and in the frieze decorations and the herms at the corners. Such female figures, as well as the curved element linking the legs, were common features of Weisweiler's work. The use of Japanese lacquer panels is characteristic of the eighteenth century.

Holland is water-country. It lies at the deltas of three great rivers – the Rhine, the Maas and the Schelde – which flow into the sea via a network of natural and man-made waterways. Water is Holland's friend and its foe. Holland's friend, because water ensures fertile soil and offers a convenient means of transport. Thanks to its advantageous position at the mouths of three major rivers, Holland has developed into a densely populated yet prosperous country – a process which began back in the Middle Ages. But water is also Holland's foe. Its low-lying areas – the coastal provinces and the province of Utrecht – are constantly exposed to flooding by the rivers and the sea. Controlling water levels was therefore a vital concern by the Middle Ages. Dikes, dams and drainage canals were built under the supervision of local water boards, which had formed into a solid network by the turn of the fourteenth century.

Master of the St. Elizabeth Panels, *The St. Elizabeth's Day flood,* c 1500, panel, each panel 127 x 110 cm

During the night of St. Elizabeth's Day 1421, storms caused extensive flooding in Holland, Zeeland and Flanders. The top right-hand corner of this painting shows water breaking through the dike at Wieldrecht and flooding a polder known as De Grote Waard. The dike gave way again a month later, and twenty-three villages, including Wieldrecht, were destroyed. The inhabitants moved to the town of Dordrecht (shown on the left), where they donated an altarpiece – of which these panels are the wings – to the Grote Kerk.

The Prince of the Netherlands, Charles V (1500 - 1558), was also King of Spain and Emperor of Germany. He believed in a centrally governed state, with a single religion - Catholicism. In 1555 he abdicated, and his son Philip II (1527 - 1598) succeeded him as King of Spain and Prince of the Netherlands. Philip maintained his father's centralist policy and thus clashed with the Dutch nobility, who sought greater independence and also objected to the strict legal restrictions on Protestants. When their petition for tolerance was rejected in 1566, the Dutch broke out in open rebellion. Churches were attacked and images of saints destroyed. This wave of iconoclasm was the start of the Dutch revolt against Philip II. The revolt was led by Prince William I of Orange, stadholder of Holland and Zeeland (1533 - 1584). After his death his sons continued the struggle, which was to last 80 years and became known as the Eighty Years' War (1568 - 1648).

Adriaen Thomasz Key (c 1544-after 1589), *William I (1533 - 1584), Prince of Orange, called William the Silent*, c 1568, panel, 48 x 35 cm

William of Orange championed freedom and tolerance and led the Dutch revolt against Philip II's harsh regime. In 1580 he was declared an outlaw, and in 1584 he was assassinated. Key lived in Antwerp, as did William at the time this picture was painted. It is therefore highly likely that the prince actually sat for his portrait. This was not always the case; instead, artists often copied existing portraits.

Frans Francken II (1581 - 1642), *Allegory on the abdication of Emperor Charles v in Brussels, 25 October 1555*, c 1620, panel, 134 x 172 cm

Charles V, seated on his throne, is stretching out his hands to his brother Ferdinand, on the left, and his son Philip, on the right. With this gesture of abdication, Germany passed to Ferdinand and Spain and the Netherlands to Philip. The women bearing standards symbolize the Emperor's Dutch, Spanish and Italian possessions. Charles V is depicted as ruler of the world, with women representing Europe, America and India and Neptune the oceans. Charles' motto was 'Plus Ultra' (= Further Yet).

<
Beggar's bowl and gourd, sixteenth century, wood and silver, diam. 8 cm

When Dutch nobles submitted their petition to Margaret of Parma in 1566, she dismissed them contemptuously as 'gueux' (French for beggars). The nobles adopted this name (in the Dutch form 'Geuzen') as a symbol of honour. At a banquet, the nobles dressed up as beggars and drank toasts of loyalty to each other from wooden beggars' bowls.

Adriaen Pietersz van de Venne (1589 - 1662), *Fishing for souls*, 1614, panel, 98 x 189 cm

Naked figures are being fished up out of the
water. In this picture, Jesus' words to his disciples
'Follow me, and I shall make you fishers of men'
are given a contemporary interpretation, with
Protestants and Catholics fishing for human souls.
The river divides the opposing camps: the Protestants (led by the Princes of Orange) on the left,
and the Catholics (led by Albert of Austria) on
the right. The trees on the Catholic side are with-
ered, while on the Protestant side they are in full
leaf.

Jug, **F. Enriquez,** Spain or Mexico, second half of sixteenth century, silver, 35 cm

Pauwels van Hillegaert (1595/1596 - 1640), *Prince Maurice at the Battle of Nieuwpoort*, panel, 82.5 x 117.5 cm

Each year a fleet from Spanish America sailed home to Spain, fully laden with silver and gold. The Dutch West India Company had set its sights on this 'silver fleet'. On his third attempt, in 1628, Vice-Admiral Piet Heyn succeeded in capturing part of the Spanish fleet off Cuba. On returning to Holland, Piet Heyn was given a hero's welcome. Among the spoils – 11.5 million florins' worth of money and goods – was this jug.

In 1600, Prince Maurice received instructions to march to Flanders with an army of 15,000 men and deal with the Dunkirk privateers, who were a constant menace to Dutch shipping. On 2 July, at the coastal town of Nieuwpoort, Maurice's army unexpectedly came across Spanish troops led by Albert of Austria. A battle was fought, and Maurice's superior strategy won the day. Hillegaert portrayed the prince in the foreground on the left.

In 1581, the States General of seven Dutch
provinces repudiated the authority of
Philip II as Prince of the Netherlands. In
1588, they established an independent
republic known as the United Provinces of
the Netherlands, comprising the seven
provinces of Holland, Zeeland, Utrecht,
Gelderland, Overijssel, Friesland and
Groningen. Although Protestantism was the
dominant religion in the new republic,
there was freedom of worship. The provinces enjoyed considerable autonomy, but
central authority was vested in the States
General, made up of representatives from
each province. The chief government official of the republic, the Grand Pensionary,
acted on behalf of the provinces and pre-
sided over meetings of the States General.
The stadholder, the Prince of Orange, was
employed by the States. His function as
commander-in-chief of the army was largely a military one. It was only in 1648, with
the signing of the Peace of Münster, that
the Dutch republic was officially recognized by Spain.

Dirck van Delen (1605 - 1671), *The great hall of the Binnenhof, The Hague, during the great assembly of the States
General in 1651*, panel, copper, 52 x 66 cm

The Great Hall (or Knights' Hall) of the Binnenhof in The Hague was only used for plenary
assemblies of the States General (i.e. meetings
attended by all the members of the provincial
States). The great assembly in 1651 was convened
to discuss the definitive constitutional status of
the republic. Van Delen depicted this assembly on
a hinged oblong copper plate which is attached to
the painting and can be swung into either of two
positions. The other side of the plate shows the
hall when it is empty.

The main source of income of the Dutch Republic was trade. In the seventeenth century, Amsterdam's function as a staple market enabled it to become established as an international trading centre. Goods from every corner of the globe were imported, stored in warehouses and re-exported. This was made possible by a well-equipped merchant fleet, a plentiful supply of cash and efficient trading organizations. In additional to their traditional Baltic trade in grain, iron and timber, the Dutch now extended to the Mediterranean, the Far East and the Americas.

Founded in 1602, the Dutch East India Company (VOC) was to become one of the world's leading trading companies in the seventeenth and eighteenth centuries. In addition to Indonesia, where the VOC had its administrative headquarters (at Batavia), the company had trading posts throughout Asia: in Persia (now Iran), India, Bengal, Ceylon (now Sri Lanka), Siam (now Thailand), Malacca (now part of Malaysia), Laos and Formosa (now Taiwan). Apart from the Chinese, the Dutch were the only nation allowed to trade with Japan. The main imports of the Dutch Republic were spices, but tea, lacquerwork, silk, porcelain and cotton were also imported.

The Dutch West India Company (WIC), founded in 1621, was far less profitable. The company, whose vessels plied routes to North and South America and West Africa, achieved its greatest successes in privateering.

Plane with attached plane-iron, Northern Netherlands, end of sixteenth century, beechwood, 10.5 x 5.6 x 16 cm; iron, 14 x 4 cm

In the late sixteenth century, attempts were made to find a north-east passage to China, via the coasts of Norway and Russia. During the expedition mounted by Willem Barents (c 1555 – 1597) in 1596, his ship (captained by Jacob van Heemskerk) became ice-bound near Novaya Zemlya. The crew of seventeen spent the winter on the island, using driftwood and materials from the ship to build 'Het Behouden Huys' ('The Safe House'). This plane, one of the carpenter's tools used on the expedition, was later found on Novaya Zemlya. Twelve survivors returned to Amsterdam in 1597, but without Barents – he died en route.

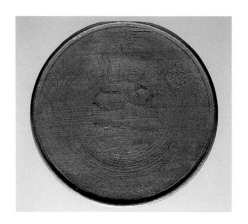

^ ^

Cornelis de Man (1621 - 1706), *The whale-oil factory on Jan Mayen Island*, 1639, canvas, 108 x 205 cm

In the first half of the seventeenth century, Jan Mayen Island and Spitsbergen were used as whaling bases by the Noordse Compagnie (Dutch Northern Company). This painting shows the company settlement on Jan Mayen Island, with the snow-clad peak known as Beerenberg in the background. In the foreground we can see the whale-oil factory in operation. On the left, a whale is being 'flensed'. On the right, the strips of blubber are being chopped up on wooden tables and boiled in huge vats. The resulting whale-oil was used for a number of different purposes.

Chopping-board and cruet, Northern Netherlands, end of sixteenth century; chopping-board, wood, diam. 20 cm; cruet, pewter, 22.4 cm

In 1597, the survivors of Willem Barents' expedition left 'The Safe House' on Novaya Zemlya, abandoning all kinds of objects on the island. Three centuries later, in 1871, a Norwegian expedition found the remains of the house and various artefacts, including weapons, clothes, books, tools and merchandise. This chopping-board and cruet were part of the tableware used on board ship.

Model of the 'Prins Willem', 1651, mainly oak and lime-wood, length (stem to stern) 103 cm

This is the oldest known model of an East India-man (a merchant vessel of the Dutch East India Company). This particular model was copied from the 'Prins Willem' (1650), named after stadholder William II (1626 – 1650). It was a large ship, some 50 metres long, with room for more than 250 crew. This scale model – one-fiftieth of actual size – provides a good deal of information about the original vessel, which was converted into a war-ship in 1652. This involved the addition of ten new guns to the thirty that the ship already car-ried.

Kendi in the form of an elephant, from the wreck of 'De Witte Leeuw', China, before 1613, porcelain, 17 cm

This kendi (Malay for jug) in the form of an elephant was used for water, with the tusks serving as spouts. The kendi is made of Chinese porcelain from the Wan-li period (1573 – 1619) and is decorated with symbols of mirth (chrysanthemums) and longevity (swastikas). It comes from 'De Witte Leeuw' (the White Lion), an East Indiaman that went down in 1613 off the island of St. Helena while returning from the Orient with a cargo of porcelain and spices. Most porcelain consisted of bowls and dishes; the kendi is an exception.

Hendrik van Schuylenburgh (c 1620 - 1689), *The factory of the Dutch East India Company at Hooghly in Bengal*, 1665, canvas, 203 x 316 cm

This picture of the Dutch East India Company trading post in Bengal is not an authentic depiction of reality, but shows different situations that prevailed there at various times. The group of buildings with the Dutch flag in one corner is the company head office, where the senior merchant and his staff lived and worked. East Indiamen are lying at anchor on the river. To the right we can see a dignitary on his way to see a local prince, who is awaiting his visitors in a nearby encampment. This painting provides a detailed record of life at the trading post.

Willem vd Velde - Krijgsraad voor den 4 daagschen zeeslag aan boord v/t Admiraalschip van M.A. de Ruyter, de Zeven Provinciën 10 Juni 1666 - Geschenk van belangstellenden 1911.

The most famous admiral in Dutch history, Michiel de Ruyter, enjoyed an international reputation and received numerous honours from other countries. De Ruyter was born in Flushing port in 1607, and first went to sea when he was only eleven years old. His navigating skills brought him rapid advancement. De Ruyter was employed by the Admiralty, in Zeeland in 1652 and in Amsterdam a year later. As vice-admiral of the fleet he took part in the numerous sea battles the Dutch fought against England. In 1665 he was appointed commander-in-chief of the Dutch fleet. He won a number of victories, but the pinnacle of his career was undoubtedly the Third Anglo-Dutch War (1672 - 1674), in which his superior tactics enabled him to keep a large Anglo-French fleet away from the Dutch coast. De Ruyter was killed at Syracuse in 1676, and was buried in the Nieuwe Kerk in Amsterdam.

Willem van de Velde I (c 1611 - 1693), *The council of war on board 'De Zeven Provinciën', the flagship of Michiel Adriaensz de Ruyter, on 10 June 1666*, 1666, canvas, 117 x 175 cm

This pen drawing by Willem van de Velde depicts the council of war on the eve of the four-day naval battle during the Second Anglo-Dutch War (1665 - 1667). The battle, which took place on 11 - 14 June 1666, was won by the Dutch fleet under De Ruyter's command. The result, however, was disappointing: the English fleet was not destroyed, and losses on the Dutch side were almost as great.

Rapier and sheath, Neapolitan, c 1676, iron, red coral, copper and leather, 104.5 cm

The unusual thing about this rapier is the carved red coral hilt. The same material was used to decorate the sheath. The Neapolitans specialized in carving coral. This magnificent item was a gift to Admiral De Ruyter from the Spanish marquis De los Veles, viceroy of Naples. He wanted to thank the Dutch for warding off the threat from the French fleet, which had defeated the Spanish at Stromboli in January 1675. Naples belonged to Spain at the time.

Arms of the King of England, part of the taffrail of the English warship 'Royal Charles', c 1664, painted pinewood, 277 x 378 cm

This coat of arms, which is held by a lion and a unicorn whose horn is missing, is part of the decoration from the taffrail (stern) of the 'Royal Charles'. Michiel de Ruyter captured this vessel and brought it back to the Netherlands following a successful attack on English ships and naval installations at Chatham (to the east of London) in June 1667. The 'Royal Charles' was broken up in 1673.

Dutch expansion overseas was in both directions, eastward and westwards. In particular, it was the establishment of the Dutch East India Company (VOC) in 1602 and the Dutch West India Company (WIC) in 1621, each with clearly demarcated areas of activity, that caused the number of Dutch overseas territories to increase rapidly. Some of the settlements in the western hemisphere were only briefly under Dutch administration: Northern Brazil (1624 - 1661) and New Holland, with the city of New Amsterdam — the future New York — at the mouth of the Hudson river (1628 - 1664). On the other hand, the islands of Curaçao, Aruba, Bonaire, St. Eustatius, Saba and St. Martin are still Dutch, while Surinam became independent in 1975.

The Far Eastern territories were the most important, including settlements in India, Ceylon (now Sri Lanka), Malacca (now part of Malaysia), Formosa (now Taiwan), the Japanese island of Deshima and the Indonesian archipelago. It was here, in Batavia on the island of Java, that the VOC established its administrative headquarters, with a governor-general in charge from 1610 onwards. Trading contracts were signed and alliances concluded with local princes.

In 1652, a staging post for VOC ships was established at the southern tip of Africa, known as the Cape of Good Hope. The arrival of settlers was to transform this into a fully-fledged Dutch colony.

Andries Beeckman (active in the Dutch East Indies c 1651 - 1657), *The castle of Batavia, seen from Kali Besar West*, 1656, canvas, 108 x 151.5 cm

In the background is the castle of Batavia, the bastion of Dutch rule in Asia. This was where the VOC's administrators lived. The governor-general is just arriving in town with his retinue. In the foreground is a market by the Kali Besar, or Great River. The Dutch built Batavia in 1619 on the site of Jakarta, which they had destroyed. Beeckman was commissioned by the VOC to paint this peaceful scene on the spot.

Jan Schreuder medallion, Sri Lanka, before 1762, gold, diam. 128 x 101 mm

This medallion was a gift from Jan Schreuder, governor of Ceylon (now Sri Lanka), to Joan Alwis Wijewardene Senewiratne, the Maha Mudaliyar or senior local official. The latter was given the medallion as a mark of gratitude for his action during the revolts which occurred in VOC-administered territories in 1760 and 1761. Ceylon was partly Dutch from 1658 to 1802.

At the beginning of the nineteenth century, when the Dutch republic was briefly governed by France, most of Holland's overseas territories passed into British hands. For many of the Asian settlements, this meant the end of Dutch rule. An exception was the Indonesian archipelago (the Dutch East Indies), which was given back to Holland in 1816. In 1830, governor-general Van den Bosch introduced what was known as the Cultuurstelsel — a system of forced farming — to help Holland out of its financial difficulties. Under this system, which was restricted to Java, the population was forced to grow lucrative export crops such as coffee, tea, sugar, tobacco and indigo (a plant which yielded a blue dye). The Dutch used native chiefs to help organize and supervise the system. In 1870, in response to mounting criticism of such exploitation, the Cultuurstelsel was abolished, and trade and industry now began to develop in the Dutch East Indies. The colony did not actually become a single political unit until about 1900, when a series of minor wars — the longest and most significant of which was the Aceh War — effectively established Dutch rule throughout the archipelago.

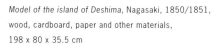

Model of the island of Deshima, Nagasaki, 1850/1851, wood, cardboard, paper and other materials, 198 x 80 x 35.5 cm

Diorama: view of the square in Paramaribo, **Gerrit Schouten,** 1812, paper, 68.5 x 99 x 32 cm

Chinese vase, presented to Jacob Theodoor Cremer, China, 1883, silver, 86 cm

This model, which was made in Nagasaki, was commissioned by Frederik Cornelis Rose (1808 – after 1858), chief of the VOC trading post on the small island of Deshima in Nagasaki Bay. From here the Dutch traded with Japan from 1641 to 1860. The Dutch were the only Europeans, and indeed the only foreigners apart from the Chinese (who operated from an adjacent islet), who were allowed to do so. Around 1860 these privileges were abolished and Japan was opened up to all foreigners.

While Holland was governed by France, Surinam fell under British rule. This diorama – a three-dimensional scene displayed in a shallow box – shows the square and the governor's palace in Paramaribo (the capital of Surinam). The British governor, Sir Pinson Bonham, and his family are just about to depart. On the right are the Surinam river and Fort Zeelandia, with the Union Jack flying.

This vase was presented to J. T. Cremer in 1883 by the planters of Deli-Langkat and Serdang on the island of Sumatra, in the Dutch East Indies. Cremer was manager of the Deli Company and made a major contribution to the success of tobacco growing in East Sumatra. As an expert on the colonies he was involved in numerous local businesses, including the Deli Railway Company and various shipping firms. After returning home to the Netherlands he was Minister of Colonial Affairs from 1897 to 1901.

Nassau tunic, 1647, linen, silk, metal thread, 86 x 125 cm

This tunic was made for the funeral of stadholder Prince Frederick Henry in 1647. It is the only surviving item from an original set of five, which were worn by heralds and had a symbolic function. The entire coat of arms of the House of Orange-Nassau was embroidered on the tunic four times. This served to display all the monarch's titles of nobility and the extent of his power. The same tunic was used at the funeral of stadholder Prince William IV in 1752.

Dressing-gown (Japanese robe) belonging to stadholder King William III (1650 - 1702), Northern Netherlands, second half of seventeenth century, padded and embroidered silk, 154 cm

This dressing-gown was worn by stadholder King William III; he and his wife Mary Stuart became King and Queen of England in 1688. The dressing-gown was made of purple silk (now yellowed with age) with a bright green lining, just like a Japanese kimono. Trade with Japan introduced the kimono into Holland, where it was known as a 'Japanese robe'. Its distinguished appearance soon made it a fashionable item, and many people had their portraits painted in a kimono.

Box in which the charter of the Dutch West India Company was presented to stadholder William IV in 1749, **Jean Saint** (1698 - 1774), probably after a design by **François Thuret** (1716 - after 1755), Amsterdam, tortoiseshell mounted with gold, 18 x 11.5 x 5 cm

The lid of this box is decorated with a gold mounting. The main illustration depicts gold mining, represented by a black man and black woman with a cornucopia full of gold ore. Mercury, the god of trade and profit, is holding a shield that bears the monogram of the Dutch West India Company. On the sides of the box are forts in overseas territories belonging to the company.

Otto Eerelman (1839 - 1926), *Arrival of Queen Wilhelmina at the Frederiksplein in Amsterdam on 5 September 1898,* canvas, 139 x 195 cm

On 6 September 1898, at the age of eighteen, Princess Wilhelmina (1880 – 1962) was officially enthroned as Queen of the Netherlands. She was the only child of King William III and Queen Emma and, following the death of her half-brother Alexander, the sole successor. She had actually succeeded her father in 1890, but her investiture in Amsterdam only took place when she reached the age of majority. Eerelman painted the scene on the day before the investiture, when Wilhelmina rode in a cream-coloured coach from Weesperpoort Station to the Royal Palace on the Dam.

Pierre-Paul Prud'hon (1758 - 1823), *Rutger Jan Schimmelpenninck with his wife and children*, 1801/1802, canvas, 263.5 x 200 cm

From 1798 to 1802, Rutger Jan Schimmelpenninck (1761 – 1825) was the envoy of the Batavian Republic (as the Netherlands was then known) in Paris. However, Prud'hon did not portray him as a diplomat but as the head of a family, with his wife Catharina Nahuys, his twelve-year-old daughter Catharina and his eight-year-old son Gerrit. Prud'hon exhibited this painting at the Salon in Paris, with the title *Réunion de famille*.

In 1813 the period of French rule came to an end, and the Netherlands recovered its independence. It was decided that the Northern and Southern Netherlands should be amalgamated into a single kingdom, as a buffer against France, with the Prince of Orange as King William I.

In 1830 the Belgians rose in rebellion. Dutch military intervention had no effect, and on 8 November 1830 Belgium declared itself independent. The new state was recognized by the great powers in 1831, and in 1839 the Netherlands finally followed suit. The year 1848 was a milestone in Dutch history: under pressure from the liberal opposition, King William II reluctantly consented to a fundamental revision of the constitution, which put an end to the sovereign's hitherto unlimited power. The Netherlands became a constitutional monarchy and, under William III and especially Queen Emma and Queen Wilhelmina, the House of Orange became a source of national unity.

Jan Willem Pieneman (1779 - 1853), *The Triumvirate assuming power on behalf of the Prince of Orange, 21 November 1813, in or shortly after 1828*, canvas, 70 x 86.5 cm

In order to assume the power relinquished by the French in 1813, a three-man provisional government was formed on behalf of the Prince of Orange under Gijsbert Karel van Hogendorp, who is shown sitting at the table. Standing next to him is the military governor of The Hague, Count van Limburg Stirum. The third member of the triumvirate, A.F.J.A. van der Duyn van Maasdam, was not actually present on that occasion, but Pieneman included him anyway: he is shown standing behind Van Hogendorp.

Jan Willem Pieneman (1779 - 1853), *The Battle of Waterloo, 18 June 1815*, 1824, canvas, 576 x 836 cm

Waterloo was Napoleon's last battle. He was defeated by a combined army of British, Dutch and Prussian troops. Pieneman depicted the decisive moment in the battle, with some of the victors prominent in the foreground: the British commander-in-chief, the Duke of Wellington, on horseback, and the Prince of Orange – the future King William II – lying wounded on a stretcher to the left. The painting was a gift to the prince from his father King William I.

Jan Hendrik Neuman, *Johan Rudolf Thorbecke (1798 - 1872), Minister of State and Minister of the Interior,* probably 1852, canvas, 100 x 84 cm

The liberal politician Thorbecke was thrice prime minister. His political career began in the 1840s. Before that he had been a professor, first at Ghent and later at the faculty of law in Leiden. Thorbecke's legislative achievements were particularly striking: the Constitution of 1848 (which was largely his work), the Electoral Act and the Provincial Act of 1850, and the Local Government Act of 1851. This portrait must have been painted at around that time, since the letter on the table is dated 1852.

Model of the Egmond lighthouse, **J. Valk,** 1840, 160 x 112 x 110 cm

This is a model of the Egmond lighthouse (actual height 25 metres), which was erected in memory of Jan Carel Josephus van Speyk (1802 – 1831). During the Ten Days' Campaign in 1831, this Dutch naval officer blew up his gunboat in Antwerp to prevent it falling into the hands of the Belgians. The monument was built on the initiative of the College Zeemanshoop.

Unknown artist, *Wilhelmina (1880 - 1962), Queen of the Netherlands (1898 - 1948),* c 1948, canvas, 281 x 191 cm

This ceremonial portrait of Queen Wilhelmina is badly slashed and stained with ink. It originally hung in the Netherlands High Commission in Jakarta, the capital of Indonesia. On 6 May 1960 the painting was vandalized during student riots which broke out when the Netherlands refused to cede Dutch New Guinea to Indonesia. Queen Wilhelmina was seen as a symbol of Dutch colonialism. The painting is now exhibited in the Rijksmuseum as a token of Holland's colonial past.

Shell portrait of Dr. Willem Drees, **W. M. Voois,** Ter Heijde, c 1960, shells, wood and linen, 26 x 29.5 x 2 cm

The socialist politician Willem Drees (1886 – 1987) was Minister of Social Affairs from 1945 to 1948. Drees was responsible for introducing Holland's first old-age pension legislation, which was passed on 25 May 1947. This was superseded by the present act on 1 January 1957. This portrait of Drees, which is made of shells, was presented to the politician by the artist as a token of gratitude for the old-age pension which Drees had made it possible for him to enjoy.

The Print Room houses the largest collection of prints and drawings in the Netherlands, the main part of which consists of the celebrated eighteenth-century collection of Pieter Cornelis Baron van Leyden (1717 - 1788), which was purchased in 1807 by the then King of Holland, Louis Napoleon. The collection includes an important group of etchings by Rembrandt, among them some unique works and numerous proofs in various states. In 1961, the group was doubled in size by a donation from Mr. and Mrs. de Bruyn, making the museum's collection of Rembrandt etchings now one of the most complete in the world. The museum also possesses a considerable number of Rembrandt's drawings. Most of these came to the museum in the form of donations – from C. Hofstede de Groot in 1931, and a smaller group from Mr. and Mrs. de Bruyn in 1961.

The Print Room now has 60 of Rembrandt's own drawings, a small number of which were purchased. In addition to a representative selection of Dutch and various foreign schools, Baron van Leyden's collection contained some more exceptional groups of prints, including extremely rare ones by the fifteenth-century Master of the Amsterdam Print Room and others by Rembrandt's contemporary Hercules Segers. The other main element in the Print Room is the collection formerly belonging to stadholder William v (1748 - 1806), including prints by Dürer, Callot and Goltzius. This collection was originally housed in the Royal Library in The Hague, but was transferred to the Rijksmuseum in 1816.

The Print Room has greatly benefited from the patronage of F.G. Waller, who, on his death in 1934, left a sufficient endowment to cover the cost of purchasing prints right up to the present day. The regular budget is now entirely used for drawings. It was not until the end of the nineteenth century that the Rijksmuseum began to collect drawings. The impetus was provided by the Rembrandt Association, which succeeded in acquiring five hundred drawings (most of them Dutch) for the Print Room when the famous collection belonging to Jacob de Vos Jbzn was auctioned in Amsterdam in 1883. Since then, the collection has developed into an overview of Dutch drawing from the sixteenth to the mid-twentieth century. Although foreign schools are less well represented, the collection includes some outstanding French eighteenth-century drawings by such artists as Watteau, Fragonard and Boucher (from the Mannheimer collection).

The collection of Italian drawings did not grow to any significant size until after the Second World War. In 1981, it was further expanded by a large bequest of over 60 drawings from the I.Q. van Regteren Altena collection. In recent years, particular efforts have been made to fill up the gaps in the museum's collection of English watercolours and drawings. The Print Room also includes a collection of Oriental graphic art, complementing the collections in the Asiatic Art department. Examples are the selection of Japanese colour woodcuts, from the Lieftinck collection, and Japanese surimonos (occasional prints) from the Bierens de Haan and Goslings collections. In 1993, an existing small group of Indian miniatures was significantly increased by a donation from the Formijne collection, with the result that the museum can now provide a broad overview of this refined, exotic art form.

In addition to prints and drawings, the Print Room also has a large number of minor collections, including a collection of decorative prints (based on the Frederiks collection), a collection of popular and children's prints and decorated paper (both donated by F.G. Waller), Frederik Muller's historical atlas, a chronological collection of prints relating to Dutch history, and a collection of portraits of stadholders and Princes of Orange. Another item is the Ottens Atlas, a collection of topographical prints which was purchased by stadholder William v in 1773. The iconographic collection, which is classified by subject, and the collection of portraits are of a more documentary nature.

Recently the range of exhibits was significantly extended to include a collection of photographs which the State acquired in the 1980s. Together with the other photographs in the museum, this collection offers a picture of Dutch and foreign photography from the nineteenth and early twentieth century.

Since works executed on paper deteriorate if exposed to light for too long, the prints and drawings are not on permanent display, but are rotated from time to time. Visitors who wish to view prints and drawings from the Print Room collection may do so, on request, in the reading room (entrance: 1A, Jan Luyken-straat).

Master of the Amsterdam Cabinet (c 1470 - c 1500), *Aristotle and Phyllis*, c 1485, dry point, diam. 155 mm

Here we see the philosopher Aristotle crawling about with the lovely Phyllis on his back, watched by two other men. Aristotle, who was allegedly indifferent to femal beauty, nevertheless let himself be enticed and, worse still, humiliated by a woman. The artist used various kinds of shading to achieve an extremely vivid rendering of this scene, which is based on a popular thirteenth-century tale. This print is among his most outstanding work.

Cornelis Anthonisz (c 1499 - c 1555), *Henry VIII of England on horseback*, c 1538, hand-coloured woodcut, 403 x 295 mm

Anthonisz painted this portrait of Henry VIII on horseback after the king had had his hair and beard cut short in 1535. The coat of arms and inscriptions make it quite clear whose portrait this is. 'Dieu et mon droit' is the motto of the British royal family. This woodcut was made in Amsterdam, but published in Antwerp by Hans Liefrinck. The colouring was added with great care. This was probably Liefrinck's first issue of the series of royal portraits by Anthonisz.

Hercules Segers (1589/1590 - 1634/1638), *Two trees*, middle of first half of seventeenth century, etching, printed in brown on paper prepared in pink and blue, 155 x 173 mm

Two trees stand out against the sky. The delicate foliage is portrayed in great detail, and in the left-hand tree we can see young twigs which have burst forth after pruning. This study of nature is a unique work by Segers, who mostly depicted fantastic landscapes. In this etching, Segers – unlike most other artists – used not only black ink, but also other colours. His etching technique enabled him to achieve very striking results – 'painting without (oil) paint'.

Federico Barocci (c 1535 - 1612), *The adoration of the Magi*, c 1561 - 1563, black chalk, pen and brush (brown, white and pale yellow) on blue paper, 293 x 209 mm

The Virgin Mary, surrounded by the three kings, is sitting with Jesus on her lap. The kings have just arrived: in the foreground we can see a horse being held by the reins, and one of the kings with his crown in his hand. Barocci used white and pale yellow to create effects of light in this lively sketch. The drawing must have been a preliminary study for a painting (which is not known to have survived). The artist's efforts to achieve an ideal composition are very apparent.

Jacques de Gheyn II (1565 - 1625), *Four studies of a frog*, early seventeenth century, pen (brown) and brush (colours), 142 x 196 mm

This is one of De Gheyn's most characteristic animal drawings. The frogs are observed with great accuracy, although only the one in the top right-hand corner is in a natural pose. It is not known whether the artist used stuffed frogs or live ones pinned in place. At the beginning of the seventeenth century there was considerable interest in faithful depictions of nature, as well as in nature itself. De Gheyn, and his tutor Hendrick Goltzius, are among the great Dutch painters of animals.

Hendrick Avercamp (1585 - 1634), *Fishermen by moonlight*, c 1620 - 1630, pen (brown) and brush (colours), 144 x 195 mm

A moonlit river, with fishermen working away busily in their boats, and a town silhouetted on the bank. Further down we can see ships being repaired; they have been careened so that their hulls can be burnt clean. The fiery glow to the right indicates more work going on. The sense of night-time is conveyed with great skill. Avercamp produced a large number of elaborate drawings such as this, which were often framed as small paintings. This is his only moonlit scene.

Jacob Marrel (1614 - 1681), *Four tulips and an anemone,*
c 1637 - 1640, coloured brushwork on parchment,
340 x 450 mm

These flowers are illustrated in extremely precise
detail, with beautiful colour transitions. Their
names are also indicated. Tulips were introduced
into Holland from Turkey at the end of the sixteenth century, and soon became very popular.
Absurd prices were paid for the bulbs, and proud
owners had their costly blooms immortalized in
paint. This is a page from one of the tulip albums
produced by the German artist Marrel, who lived
in Utrecht from 1634 to 1649. He was also a deal-
er in tulips.

Jacob Cats (1741 - 1799), *Autumn landscape with rainbow*, 1779, watercolour and pen (brown), 334 x 415 mm

A typically Dutch landscape: stormy weather, driving rain, lashing waves, a lock, and water flooding over the dike into the polder below. In apparent desperation, the man on the lock has joined his hands in prayer, and elsewhere cattle are being driven up onto the dike. This autumn landscape is one of a series depicting the four seasons, together with the four quarters of the day and the four elements – in this case, afternoon and water. Not long after Cats' death, this series was already acknowledged to be his masterpiece.

Rembrandt van Rijn (1606 - 1669), *Boaz casting barley into Ruth's veil*, c 1645, pen (brown) and brush (white), 126 x 143 mm

Boaz confirmed his promise to marry Ruth by casting barley into her veil. Ruth, who had come to Canaan with her mother-in-law Naomi, had gone out into Boaz' fields to glean ears of corn, and had spent the night lying at his feet. Rembrandt conveyed this scene from the Book of Ruth with broad, contrasting strokes. He omitted the background altogether – what mattered to him were the figures and their expressions.

Thomas Gainsborough (1727 - 1788), *Six studies of a cat*, 1765 - 1770, black and white chalk on grey paper, 310 x 447 mm

A cat in typically feline poses: alert, half-asleep, curled up snugly, and washing itself at great length. These cats by the English painter Gainsborough are extremely lifelike. This chalk drawing is unusual for him, for he seldom portrayed animals – most of his drawings were of landscapes and people. Tradition has it that the artist produced this drawing as a gift to his hostess while staying at her home. This would seem to be confirmed by the signature, for Gainsborough did not normally sign his drawings.

Jean-Honoré Fragonard (1732 - 1806), *Young woman standing*, c 1775 - 1785, red chalk, 380 x 242 mm

Opinions differ as to the identity of this young woman, who is shown elegantly gathering up her skirts. It could be Fragonard's sister-in-law and pupil Marguerite Gérard or, as is nowadays believed, his daughter Rosalie. Fragonard took full advantage of his material, chalk, using a variety of contours, planes and shading to produce a charming portrait. His rendering of the satin material and the facial expression is particularly masterly.

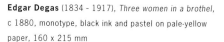

Anton Mauve (1838 - 1888), *The wagon*, 1885, water-colour, 420 x 575 mm

The painters of the Hague School took their sub-jects from nature. Anton Mauve mainly chose the coastal dunes and the sheep that grazed there. In 1885, the urban sprawl of The Hague forced him to move to Laren, a still unspoilt farming village to the north of Utrecht. It was here that he pro-duced this watercolour of a wagon with two large wheels. The dank atmosphere of the area – not far from what was then the Zuiderzee – is particularly well conveyed.

Edgar Degas (1834 - 1917), *Three women in a brothel*, c 1880, monotype, black ink and pastel on pale-yellow paper, 160 x 215 mm

Three prostitutes in a brothel. The French paint-er Degas portrayed the women in almost pitiless close-up. It seems as if the artist drew them on the spot, but in fact he produced this brothel scene at home, in his studio, as a monotype. Monotype is a printing technique in which the picture is inked directly onto the plate. In total, Degas produced some fifty brothel scenes, all monotypes. Only six were coloured in with pastels.

Gustave Le Gray (1820 - 1882), *The royal yacht 'La Reine Hortense' in Le Havre*, c 1856, albumen print, 325 x 413 mm

This photograph of the royal yacht in Le Havre harbour is the first of a series of pictures of harbours, ships, rigging and seascapes. Le Gray photographed the ship against a plain sky, paying attention to every detail. Even the faces of the people on board are clearly distinguishable. Le Gray, who was one of France's leading nineteenth-century photographers, trained many others.

Eduard Isaac Asser (1809 - 1894), *Portrait of one of the photographer's daughters*, c 1855, photograph, salt-paper print from collodion glass negative, gold-tinted, 151 x 111 mm

Photography was invented in the nineteenth century. At first only a few people took an interest in it, and there was a good deal of experimentation. Eduard Asser, of Amsterdam, was a typical inventor – a 'gentleman photographer'. A lawyer by profession, he instantly made photography his hobby, mainly producing portraits of relatives and friends. This portrait of his daughter was taken after his 'experimental period', when he was already an experienced photographer.

George Hendrik Breitner (1857 - 1923), *The Oudezijds Achterburgwal in Amsterdam*, c 1895, platinotype, 299 x 348 mm

Breitner is particularly famous for his impressionist paintings of Amsterdam, which vividly depict city life. He often based these paintings on photographs, in combination with sketches and notes. As far as is known, no painting was ever made from this photograph of the Oudezijds Achterburgwal. The photograph is one of a series of 60 enlargements. Breitner was an extremely prolific photographer: thousands of negatives were found among his belongings after he died.

Struggle between Krishna and Shrigala, Mogul miniature, India, end of sixteenth century, brush (colour and gold) on paper, 427 x 275 mm (including border)

This is an illustration from the Harivamsha, one of the Hindu holy books. The book relates the life of Krishna, an incarnation of the Hindu god Vishnu. This print shows the struggle between Krishna, identifiable by his blue skin (on the left), and his adversary Shrigala (on the right), who has just been decapitated – his head is lying on the ground. This colourful, detailed portrayal is an important example of court art under the Great Mogul Akbar (1556 – 1605).

Utagawa Kuniyoshi (1798 - 1861), *View of the island of Tsukuda*, c 1833, colour woodcut, 242 x 363 mm

The island of Tsukuda, with fishing-boats at anchor, can be seen between the pillars of a bridge. Two women are being rowed across to the island. The scraps of paper drifting down from the bridge add a lively note. Kuniyoshi was a versatile artist. At first he concentrated on traditional Japanese subjects, but in the 1830s he shifted to other themes. A striking feature is his use of such Western elements as perspective and shadow.

Although Oriental art has been part of the Rijksmuseum collection for as long as the museum has existed, the Asiatic Art department is the youngest section of the museum. While all the other departments also collect Oriental art, they do so - with the exception of the Print Room - from a different point of view. The Print Room includes Japanese graphic art and Indian miniatures. The Dutch History department exhibits objects which say something about the Dutch in Asia. The Sculpture and Decorative Arts department has allocated an entire room to art produced in Asia but commissioned by Dutch people who lived there, with European forms but Asiatic workmanship: 'colonial art'. The Paintings department only includes illustrations of Oriental art, such as Chinese porcelain plates in still lifes. The Asiatic Art department, on the other hand, collects and exhibits Asiatic art for its own sake.

The department stems from several different collections: the collection belonging to the Association of Friends of Asiatic Art, the collection of Asiatic art built up by the department since 1965, and the Oriental items from the Sculpture and Decorative Arts department.

The Association of Friends of Asiatic Art was set up in 1918 in order to foster a better understanding of Asiatic art. One of the ways in which it has pursued this goal is collecting works of art. Starting in 1932, the Association's collection was exhibited in the garden room of the Amsterdam Municipal Museum, and so became accessible to the public. In 1952 the collection was transferred to the South Wing of the Rijksmuseum, together with a generous selection of the Chinese porcelain owned by the museum. Up to 1965, the Association's collection continued to be a separate entity known as the Museum of Asiatic Art. From 1965 to 1972, the Museum of Asiatic Art was transferred in stages to a department of the Rijksmuseum, with its own curator and purchasing funds. In 1972 the collec-

tion was given to the Rijksmuseum on permanent loan, to be exhibited in the Asiatic Art department. Most of the Oriental art in the Sculpture and Applied Art department is Chinese porcelain from the seventeenth to nineteenth century, plus a small amount of Japanese lacquerwork. Porcelain and lacquer were the two Oriental products which reached Europe before the seventeenth century, arousing great admiration and even becoming standard features of Dutch domestic interiors. An interesting example is the collection built up in the second half of the eighteenth century by J.T. Royer (1737 - 1808), an amateur sinologist from The Hague.

Since porcelain and lacquer only give a very limited impression of the works of art produced in Asia, the Association of Friends of Asiatic Art has endeavoured to focus attention on other types of Asiatic art which are considered important in Asia itself. The same aim has been adopted by the Asiatic Art department. This means that the department has concentrated on works of art from regions of Asia which are considered to offer outstanding or characteristic examples of major artistic trends or developments in style. These regions are East Asia (China, Japan and Korea), South Asia (India, Pakistan, Bangladesh and Sri Lanka), the Himalayas (Tibet and Nepal) and South-East Asia (Burma, Cambodia, Thailand, Vietnam and Indonesia).

The collection includes such splendid items as the twelfth-century Chinese polychromed wood carving of the bodhisattva Guanyin, sitting in a relaxed pose (p. 168); a statue of the Hindu god Shiva, Lord of the Dance, which is a magnificent specimen of high-quality bronze casting under the South Indian Cola dynasty (p. 171); and a twelve-page album by the unconventional artist Gao Qipei (1662 - 1734), who painted pictures with his fingers and fingernails (p. 167).

The bodhisattva Guanyin with lotus, China, 512, gilded bronze, height 17.5 cm

Lotuses feature prominently in this delicately sculpted statuette. The halo behind the Buddhist deity Avalokiteshvara (known in Chinese as Guanyin) is in the shape of a lotus petal, and the god is standing on an inverted lotus flower. In his right hand he is holding a lotus with closed petals. The lotus symbolizes birth and vitality. In Guanyin's hand it refers to his creative power, while the lotus he is standing on points to his divine birth.

Tripod (ding), China, thirteenth to twelfth century B.C., bronze, height 23 cm
On loan from the Association of Friends of Asiatic Art

This three-legged bronze cooking pot, which is about 3,200 years old, was probably used in rituals. It is decorated with geometric forms suggesting monsters' heads and dragons. These forms appear in relief on the surface of the pot, which is also encircled with a ring of fifteen stylized cicadas (a kind of grasshopper).

Hexagonal box, China, seventh or eighth century, partly gilded silver, diameter 11.5 cm
On loan from the Association of Friends of Asiatic Art

Silver boxes from the Tang period (late seventh to early eighth century) are by no means rare, but this specimen is particularly well executed. It is in the shape of a flower with six petals, each decorated with golden flower and bird motifs. It is not known what was kept in the box.

Gao Qipei (1660 - 1734), *Landscape with waterfall,* late seventeenth to early eighteenth century, China, ink and light colours on paper, 27.2 x 33.2 cm
On loan from the Association of Friends of Asiatic Art

Gao Qipei produced this painting with his fingers and fingernails, using loose, sketch-like strokes to portray this house on a rock above a waterfall. Sheer mountains stand out against the distant sky. The art of finger painting was practised in China from the end of the seventeenth century onwards. Gao Qipei was the first important artist in this field. A senior government official as well as a painter, he produced thousands of finger paintings.

Porcelain bottle, China, early fifteenth century, porcelain, height 45 cm

The two flat sides of this bottle are decorated with cobalt-blue branches, blossoms and foliage. The decoration is covered with a transparent eggshell glaze. The blue cobalt pigment was probably imported from Persia, but the decoration of stylized peonies, lotuses and chrysanthemums is typically Chinese.

From the Ming period (1368 – 1487) onwards, this type of porcelain became a popular export. It was considered a luxury in countries far beyond China's borders. This particular bottle was found on the Moluccan island of Halmahera, in the Indonesian archipelago.

Bodhisattva Avalokiteshvara (in Chinese: *Guanyin*), China, twelfth century, wood with traces of polychrome and gold, height 117 cm
On loan from the Association of Friends of Asiatic Art

The bodhisattva Avalokiteshvara, the Merciful, is greatly loved in the Buddhist world. He is venerated as the Great Helper, who helps the faithful to find the path to salvation and to shake off earthly ties. The bodhisattva is sitting in a significant pose. His left hand is leaning on the ground, while his right hand is resting on his knee: 'the great prince taking a rest'.

Two screens; Winter and Spring, Japan, Anonymous painter of the Unkoku school, c 1630 - 1660, colours on paper gilded with gold leaf, 166.5 x 357 cm (each)
On loan from the Association of Friends of Asiatic Art

This type of screen was used to screen off part of a Japanese room and to add a touch of colour to what were otherwise austere Japanese interiors. Japanese painters used these large surfaces to create works of art of unusual beauty and simplicity. Typical features of the Unkoku school are the way in which waves are depicted - vertically - and the sprigs of blossom which disappear beyond the edges of the picture only to reappear again elsewhere.

Altar pendant (keman), Japan, thirteenth century, gilded bronze, height 31.5 cm
On loan from the Association of Friends of Asiatic Art

Buddhist temples were traditionally decorated with garlands of flowers for festive occasions. In Japan, from the eleventh century onwards, the garlands were superseded by more durable leather or bronze decorations in the form of a fan. In reference to their origin, the fans were decorated with flowers and, in some cases, birds. Hanging down over them is a ribbon in a beautifully tied bow, looking just like fabric but actually made of bronze.

Agastya (Shiva Guru), Indonesia, c ninth century, volcanic rock, height 100 cm
On loan from the Association of Friends of Asiatic Art

Agastya is a Hindu deity. His fat belly and beard emphasize his wisdom: he is a guru, a divine teacher. The halo behind his head symbolizes his divinity. This sculpture stood in a Javanese temple dedicated to Shiva. That Agastya was a disciple of Shiva's can be seen from the trident by his side and from his other attributes: the prayer beads, the water jar and the fly whisk hanging over his left shoulder.

Buddha Shakyamuni, India or Sri Lanka, seventh or eighth century, bronze and gold, height 42 cm
On loan from the Association of Friends of Asiatic Art

This buddha is wearing a simple monk's habit which clings closely to his body, outlining its form. One of the distinguishing features of a buddha is the ushnisha, the knot of hair on top of his head. This gold ushnisha was added later – the original knot has disappeared. Bronze buddhas in this style were found in various places throughout South-East Asia. They were exported from India and Sri Lanka. This particular sculpture was found in Eastern Java, Indonesia.

Shiva, Lord of the Dance, India, twelfth century, bronze, height 154 cm
On loan from the Association of Friends of Asiatic Art

Shiva is the god of both creation and destruction. This is shown by his attributes: Shiva is using the drum in his upper right hand to beat out the rhythm of creation, while the fire in his left hand can be used to destroy the world. Shiva's other hands symbolize his third function: preserver of the world. This sculpture was carried aloft during processions, using staves which passed through the rings attached to the base.

Three-headed Vishnu, Kashmir, second half of eighth or early ninth century, dark-green stone, height 64 cm

This sculpture of the Hindu god Vishnu has not survived the passage of time unscathed. The legs and four arms have been broken off, but the three heads and the powerful chest are well preserved. As well as a human face, Vishnu has a boar's and a lion's head. As a lion and a boar, Vishnu restored the balance between good and evil. His function was to preserve the universe.

Vajravarahi, North-East India or Nepal, twelfth century, bronze inlaid with brass and silver, height 9 cm
On loan from the Association of Friends of Asiatic Art

The Buddhist goddess Vajravarahi looks like a demon. She is grinning a devilish grin and brandishing a cleaver, while in her left hand she is holding a cranium. The goddess is surrounded by symbols of death. There are skulls hanging from her belt and her necklace, and her diadem also includes five tiny skulls. The goddess's left leg would originally have been standing on a corpse.

Durga killing the buffalo demon, Bangladesh, eleventh century, stone (phyllite), height 77.5 cm

The popular Hindu goddess Durga is using one of her eight arms to kill the buffalo demon, which is emerging from the neck of a buffalo that Durga has just decapitated. Durga was the only one who could defeat this demon, and she had a weapon in each hand. The other gods had given her the weapons so that she could do battle with evil. This relief was originally built into the wall of a brick temple.

Avalokiteshvara, Nepal, fourteenth or fifteenth century, bronze with traces of gilt, semi-precious stones, height 23.2 cm
On loan from the Association of Friends of Asiatic Art

Avalokiteshvara is a Buddhist god who is very popular because he can help the faithful with all their problems. He is wearing a tall crown with a monster's head on the front. His crown, necklace, bracelets and belt-buckle are decorated with semi-precious stones. Avalokiteshvara is holding the stalk of a lotus flower between the fingers of his left hand. The flower, which has since disappeared, must once have wound its way up the god's arm all the way to his shoulder.

Storage jar, Vietnam, fifteenth century, stoneware, blue
decoration covered with transparent glaze, height 30 cm

This Vietnamese storage jar is decorated with
peonies and gracefully curving plant tendrils. Originally it must have had a lid, which was held in
place by the four little handles near the top of the
jar. The shape of the jar and the flower decoration were inspired by Chinese porcelain made a
century earlier, in the Yuan period (1279 – 1368).

Flagon, Korea, twelfth or thirteenth century, porcelain-type
stoneware, gold lacquer repair (old), height 34 cm
On loan from the Association of Friends of Asiatic Art, Wes-
tendorp bequest

This wine flagon was decorated by means of the
Korean inlay technique known as sanggam: decorations were cut into the surface and then filled
up with black and white clay paste. This was covered with a greyish-green celadon glaze. Vertical
grooves divide the flagon into eight segments,
each of which is decorated with chrysanthemums.
The chrysanthemum was a favourite ornamental
motif in Korean ceramics and lacquerwork.